((Collins *rambl*

chilterns & ridge[way]

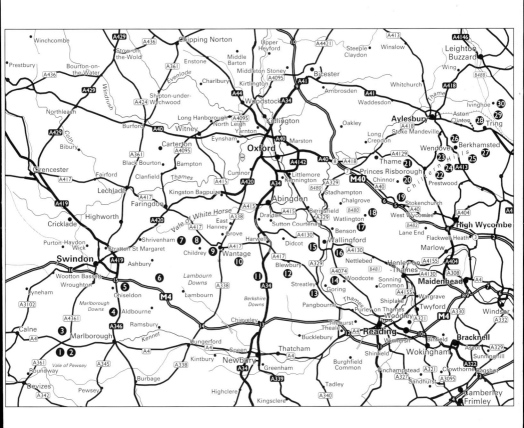

The Ramblers

Martin Andrew

HarperCollins*Publishers*
77–85 Fulham Palace Road
London W6 8JB

The HarperCollins website address is:

www.**fire**and**water**.com

06 05 04 03 02 01

10 9 8 7 6 5 4 3 2 1

First published 2001

Series Editor Richard Sale

We are grateful to the following members of the Ramblers' Association who kindly
assisted in checking the walks in this book: Jane Annett, J Archer, Linda Ashwell, Eileen
Berger, Rona Bingham, David Bradnack, Keith Brown, Roy Burton, John Cassells, A and
M Coles, Joan and Derek Crosbee, John Esslemont, John Gordon, Jane Boddington, C R
Hart, Angie Higgs, Arthur and Eileen Hutt, Margaret and Jack Ibbott, N T Jones, Audrey
Moring, Joy Payne, P Roe, John Rowe, J Smith, K Tibbs, David Trease, J White.

ISBN 0 00 710618 1

Designed and produced by Drum Enterprises Ltd.
Printed and bound in Great Britain by Scotprint

CONTENTS

INTRODUCTION

The Ridgeway Path, 85 miles (137km) long, follows one of the great chalk ranges that give southern and south-east England their main uplands, all converging on Wiltshire. Although never over 1,000 ft above sea level, the ranges covered in this book, the Marlborough Downs, the Berkshire Downs and the Chiltern Hills have some spectacular scenery, particularly along the northern escarpment where there are splendid long views over the clay vales. This book gives the walker 30 excellent circular walks ranging in distance from five to 17 miles, all of which incorporate elements of the Ridgeway Path in varying lengths. They aim to put the hill route it follows into a broader context and in most of the walks the routes descend into the vale below (and consequently climb back out). So despite their relative modesty in the height stakes compared with other volumes in the series, the walks make the most of the escarpment and the steep-sided, dry valleys south of the Ridge.

The Ridgeway Path follows ancient trackways along part of the chalk hills that dominate the south-east of England. In fact the extent of the chalk is very considerable, finally disappearing into the sea at Flamborough Head in Yorkshire. Heading south it forms the Yorkshire Wolds and then the Lincolnshire Wolds. It disappears under the Wash to reappear as much lower hills through Norfolk and Suffolk, before curving south-west into north Essex and Bedfordshire to become the Chilterns, the Berkshire Downs and the Marlborough Downs. Here it joins the great chalk plains of central Wiltshire and Salisbury Plain with ranges of chalk heading off south-west into Dorset, and eastward to form the North and South Downs which both disappear into the English Channel, before reappearing in northern France.

The chalk layer, varying in thickness between 300ft and 500ft (91m and 152m) was formed in warm, shallow seas some 60 million years ago. It comprised the sediment mainly from planktonic algae, with lesser proportions of microscopic fossils and shell fragments. Within, are bands of flints, hard silica nodules and in some areas sarsen stones, which seem to be the remains of sand layers percolated by silica to form very, very hard stone. Sarsens litter the western Marlborough Downs, also appearing in the Chilterns around High Wycombe as Denner Hill stone.

Geological forces folded the chalk rock into domes and ridges, which over millions of years eroded away to produce the escarpments. In effect, the erosion front with the dip, slopes behind the surviving top surface of the chalk. In areas there are large areas of clay with flints overlying the chalk, particularly in the Chilterns, which produce a richer pasture land but more muddy walking.

The Ridgeway Path National Trail, mostly opened in 1972, starts just north of East Kennett in Wiltshire and heads north and east fairly consistently along the crest of the chalk escarpment of the Marlborough Downs and then the Berkshire Downs, descending to the River Thames at Goring. In the Chilterns it follows the ridge where possible, but there are stretches along an equally ancient route, the Icknield Way, and even along an Anglo-Saxon earthwork between the Thames and Nuffield, Grim's Ditch. This is partly because, for some stretches, there is no clear escarpment and the hills are too diffuse, but it ends with a flourish along the Pitstone Hills to Ivinghoe Beacon.

The start of it all: The Ridgeway Path at West Overton

It is perfectly feasible to extend the Ridgeway in both directions, indeed the first walk in the book does that for four miles south of the end of the official route. There are some who would advocate extending the official route to at least the Vale of Pewsey and I have walked this stretch many times or even extending it beyond to the Dorset coast. The possibilities are endless. Although the official path covers some of the best of the Ridgeway, it must be borne in mind that the ancient Ridgeway stretched from the cliffs above Lyme Regis in Dorset to Goring, much of the southern part walkable as the Wessex Ridgeway, a path developed and waymarked by the Ramblers' Association. East of Goring, the Icknield Way, already followed intermittently by the Ridgeway Path, can be followed as far as the Countryside Agency's long distance path, the Peddar's Way, which follows the chalk north to the edge of the Wash near Hunstanton in Norfolk.

However, the best chalk landscape is undoubtedly on the official Ridgeway Path. And what a landscape it is; so very different on each side of the River Thames. Broadly speaking the open downs are west of the river with sweeping, rolling landscape, far fewer trees and vast fields on the tops and in the valleys. Pasture on the whole is confined to the steeper slopes of the sides of dry valleys and along the escarpment itself. To the east of the river, even the escarpment is wooded for much of its length and the dip slopes are also extensively wooded, the landscape altogether more intimate. Mind you, strip the woods and there are plateaux, just as there are west of the river. The difference is the greater population of the Chilterns with far more in the way of hamlets and villages and lanes linking them. On the Marlborough and Berkshire Downs there are few valleys and virtually all are dry. In the Chilterns there are rivers, the Chess, the Misbourne, the Wye and the Bulbourne. The water table is higher east of the Thames and there are more valley gravel deposits. Of course, it is easy to say that the Chilterns are tree clad because of the chair industry based in High Wycombe, and this does have a bearing, but it is also apparent that beech woods were at one time all along the Downs. Woodland ebbs and flows with changing farming and the Chilterns were once less tree covered than now, but more of that later.

On many stretches of the Ridgeway Path, the chalk juts through the soil so that the trackways are often white, the hedges are spattered with white dried up chalk thrown up by trail bikes, quad bikes and four-wheel drive vehicles. It is evidently good arable land and when grazed produces splendid springy downland turf. The escarpment is rounded rather than vertical and turf or woods cling to it: you have to wait for the sea at Beachy Head, the Seven Sisters, the Needles or Flamborough Head to get chalk cliffs (apart from the odd quarry). This gives

Winter sunlight and snow

a rippling wave-like feel to the scarp, seen to spectacular effect along the north edge of the Vale of Pewsey in both directions from Adam's grave (Walk 1). The thin turf can be stripped to expose the chalk and make enormous silhouettes, often of horses, but further south near Fovant in Wiltshire there are regimental badges or giant hill figures, like that at Cerne Abbas.

Villages and hamlets are mostly along the valley bottoms and sparse in the west. In the Chilterns there are quite a few hilltop and plateau villages such as Cholesbury, Stokenchurch or Nuffield. The size of these villages is actually quite small, often little more than hamlets with a church, such as Ipsden, Radnage, Little Hampden or The Lee. Bigger villages and towns are in the major valleys or passes through the chalk hills, such as Princes Risborough, Great Missenden, Goring or Wallingford. To the west the biggest settlements are only villages such as the Ilsleys, or the Ogbournes, and the landscape seems vaster, more lonely and less peopled. The Chilterns feel more occupied and more intimate in scale and less rugged than the Downs: this might be partly down to the smaller fields, more valleys on the dip slope and above all more wood. In some parts of the Downs the only trees seen are remote clumps amid the prairies.

It was not always so: the Anglo-Saxon name for the Berkshire Downs was 'Aescedun', the ash tree down or hills. Indeed the area covered by this walk includes some of the oldest surviving structures in England. These are grouped at the west end with Avebury their undoubted centre and feature greatly in Walks 1, 2 and 3. Here in the Neolithic era, the New Stone Age, settled life arrived with the hills and valleys farmed and great religious sites built and rebuilt indicative of surplus to pay for a priestly caste and an aristocracy. The sanctuary, for example seems to have had at least three phases of construction, some of the burial monuments were used and reused, for example East Kennett Long Barrow and Wayland's Smithy, large funerary mounds being built over smaller earlier ones. Life was not always peaceful and, I suspect, highly volatile and causeway camps were constructed on the hills for shelter and secure trading, such as on Knap Hill in Walk 1.

This was the era of the Beaker Folk, a sophisticated culture that thrived around 2,000 BC and must have cleared huge areas of woodland for cultivation. Stonehenge is obviously one of the most important Neolithic monuments, but the area covered by the first three walks is, to me, the equal in sheer wonderment at the astonishing survivals of that period. Avebury, with its stone circle and deep ditch and rampart; the ceremonial Avenue, which is over a mile and a half long and flanked once by alternately wide and tall – possibly representing males and females – and finally, the Sanctuary, more stone circles and timber ones, all set the mind racing. For ritual use, dedicatory burials have been found at the base of some of the stones. The vast scale of the enterprise and the human resources needed to achieve it, the equivalent of medieval cathedral building and all that entailed, give some kind of glimpse of a highly organised society.

All around this area, the nobility and priesthood were buried and some of the finest tombs survive in recognisable form. Evidently, it was important to be buried in the vicinity of these great sacred sites: there are for example over 5,000 tumuli within a relatively short range of Stonehenge. The best by far of these Neolithic burial monuments is West Kennett Long Barrow, which is over 340ft (103m) long and 75ft (22.7m) wide, roughly, I suppose, coffin-shaped. The burial chambers are at the broader end, shielded by a screen of sarsen stones. Within, is a passage lined with sarsens and dry-stone walling, as well as two side chambers and an end one, the roof is made of massive sarsen slabs. Actually, to enter a Neolithic structure is a remarkable experience. This might be the best monument, but Adam's Grave atop an outlier beside the Ridgeway north of Alton Barnes, must have raised spirits the highest, while Wayland's Smithy, also with a sarsen stone screen, is romantically located and hidden behind tall beech trees.

Sarsen stones feature greatly in any consideration of the period and one suspects that the sarsen fields on Fyfield and Overton Down, for example on Walk 3, seemed deeply mysterious to Neolithic peoples: building blocks from the gods perhaps. Certainly they used this intractable material in all their religious sites and it is still possible to catch feint echoes of that awe amid the stones of Avebury, despite the huge numbers of visitors drawn here. Most are relatively silent in their presence and I can see how the numinousness of ancient religious sites percolates even into our modern cynical minds. The most mysterious monument though is Silbury Hill a gigantic man-made hill 130ft (39.4m) high and 550ft (167m) wide at the base tapering to 100ft (30.3m) at the flat top. It was built in four stages from about 2,500 BC but does not appear to have been a burial mound. It must have had a major ritual significance for such colossal labour to be expended, but what was it? The Neolithic past is the focus of Walks 1, 2, 3 which cover the Avebury area and Walk 6 for Wayland's Smithy, but also crops up occasionally further east, as in the burial mound on Whiteleaf Hill in the Buckinghamshire Chilterns in Walk 22.

The Bronze Age is represented on these walks by bowl and disk barrows which occur all along the Downs and the Chilterns in varying numbers, for example at Beacon Hill on Walk 23. Also the earliest field system earthworks survive from this period, small square fields divided by banks and known as 'Celtic', although this is perhaps not entirely accurate. These systems used to survive in large areas of pasture, but ploughing has removed masses of them and you have to go to Dorset to see hundreds of acres of these ancient fields. They do crop up on several of the walks in this book, for example on Fyfield Down in Walk 3 and on Streatley Warren on Walk 13. The most important monument from this era is the Uffington White Horse, a stylised horse figure formed around 1,000 BC, and a quite remarkable survival but again why? Was it a territorial marker, a symbol of conquerors, or did it serve some ritual function?

The lusher Chilterns: near Pulpit Hill

The next major historical phase that has left its mark on the Downs and in the Chilterns is the Iron Age with its superb chain of hillforts along the Ridgeway Path. These are large enclosures surrounded by defensive ramparts and ditches with defended entrances. Nowadays of course they are earthworks, but when built they often had the ramparts faced with sarsen stones and topped by timber stockades. Many of the walks feature them and I will pick out a few for specific mention: Liddington Castle at the hinge of the Marlborough Downs where they turn east, a wind blown site with superb views across to the Cotswolds, Uffington Castle above the White Horse, and Blewburton Hill on an outlier from the main ridge. In the Chilterns there are few along the Ridgeway Path, Boddington Hill, near Wendover, Pulpit Hill, Cholesbury Camp and Ivinghoe being examples. Others are further south as though threats came from south of the Thames, rather than north of the Downs.

Nettlebed's last surviving pot kiln

The hillforts also show the need to defend (or contain) settled landscapes and it seems likely that many of the modern or at least medieval parishes perpetuate ancient estates. The classic Chiltern and Downland strip parish may be evolved from Iron Age landed estates. Why change a winning formula? The strip parish had something of everything in terms of land-use: arable open fields in the fertile heavier soils of the clay vale, a settlement or farm on the spring line at the foot of or near the escarpment, pasture or open downland on the escarpments and beyond the ridge itself, then on the dip slope seasonal pasture, woodland or daughter settlements, moors and commons. By holding a strip across all of this, a community or estate in a subsistence economy could have access to most sorts of useful land to sustain itself. The walks in this book will give an idea of how these settlements and their environs worked and recent research pushes the origins of many back into the Iron Age, if not earlier.

In the Chilterns, the Ridgeway Path actually follows stretches of the Upper Icknield Way, an ancient trackway as old as the Ridgeway, which runs from Goring to the north Norfolk coast. Below the escarpment the Romans developed what is now the Lower Icknield Way, also followed by the Ridgeway Path in parts, nearer the spring line and linking scarp foot settlements which presumably predated the road construction.

There are several good stretches of strip parishes in this book, for example in the Chilterns, Aston Clinton, Buckland and Drayton Beauchamp in Walks 27 and 28, and in the Berkshire Downs, the manors and villages between Idstone and Sparsholt on Walks 6, 7 and 8. The concept of continuity from the Iron Age, if not before, does not mean the villages and farmsteads necessarily existed then in their present locations: it is an axiom of landscape studies that settlement is fluid and the villages of today have probably only coalesced into their present form and location since the 12th or 13th Century. The tenurial, or land holding unit, is what seems to have a phenomenally long history.

The Roman conquest in the 1st Century AD found a settled landscape in the Chilterns and the Downs. Some Roman roads were driven through, one up the Og valley (Walk 4) from Mildenhall near Marlborough to Wanborough where it merged with the road from Silchester to Cirencester, later known as the Ermin Way, and further east a Roman road went through the Goring gap from Silchester to Towcester. The Tring Gap was also a key Roman route, with Akeman Street from London to Cirencester routed through it. The Romans also built many minor roads further east and as mentioned above appear to have constructed the Lower Icknield Way. Most of these roads began as military ones imposed on a pre-existing network of trackways linking settlements and farmsteads. The people probably continued unaffected to some extent with just some smarter clothes, better pottery and imported tools and artefacts. Improved farming techniques and Romanising of the upper classes and prosperous farmers resulted in some of the estates along the foot of the chalk hills having versions of Roman villas, complete with bath houses and the small fields became larger. There was a Roman villa at Woolstone (Walk 7) and elsewhere, but the impact of Rome on these hills was not as great as elsewhere, as far as visible structures are concerned: these arrive with the Anglo-Saxons.

With the arrival of Germanic invaders and the collapse of Roman administration a new phase arrives for the Ridgeway Path surroundings. The story of the conquest is not to be told here, but the Chilterns owes its name to this phase, the 'Cilternsaete', the Saxon people of Chiltern which was probably centred on Aylesbury and colonised the Chiltern Hills to the south. Berkshire emerged 'Bearruc Scir and the Saxons further west established Wilsaetan, later the basis of Wiltshire. The ferment of the first few centuries of occupation, conquest and carving out territories probably did not dramatically change the estate boundaries and these became the basis for the later emergence of the parish and manorial system, sometimes with entirely new Saxon settlers, sometimes with the landlords and officials replaced by Saxons, in other areas with the retention of Britons as slaves and labourers. The picture is still emerging from archaeology but, as ever, it is complex and ambiguous.

Nevertheless, the so-called Dark Ages appear to have given us some of the finest linear earthworks in the country. I say 'appear' advisedly as current theories are to some extent just that, as archaeology slowly fills in the gaps. The new tribal areas and sub-kingdoms seem to have felt the need of substantial physical boundaries for defence and demarcation. The most well-known, of course, is that marking the west boundary of the Kingdom of Mercia, Offa's Dyke. In the area covered in this book there are two such earthworks: Wansdyke in the west and Grim's Ditch east of the River Thames. The names are the same for 'Wan' is Woden and Grim is another name for this great Saxon god. The names presumably come from a later phase in Anglo-Saxon history when these mighty works were seen as the work of gods. Wansdyke is particularly impressive in open country as seen in Walk 1 and less so in the woods in Walk 2. Grim's Ditch runs intermittently from the Thames near Wallingford to The Hampdens (Walk 24) to Pitstone (Walk 30), mostly within woodland, and is evidently not a defensive rampart as the ditch is on the uphill side. These great earthworks, a rampart and a ditch, are matched by the Anglo-Saxon town of Wallingford, one of Alfred the Great's 'burhs', or walled towns, established to defend Wessex from the Danes, whose 9th-Century defensive ramparts and ditch survive to a remarkable extent.

Moving on to medieval times, the parish system became established by the 13th Century with the boundaries normally following those of pre-Norman estates. This can be demonstrated where Anglo-Saxon land charters survive with the boundaries described. Dr Arnold Baines has worked on many of these, such as Monks Risborough in Buckinghamshire, which dates to the 10th Century, whose bounds coincide with that of the medieval ecclesiastical parish (Walk 22). This is interesting because this parish was a typical long, narrow parish, stretching from the clay vale with Monks Risborough on the spring line, the parish continuing south up the escarpment and down the dip slope. Further along, on the Berkshire Downs the former parish boundaries of the villages, hamlets, and single farms can be traced clearly, although many are no longer parishes. From the Wiltshire border east there is a long line of strip parishes: Idstone, Ashbury, Kingstone, Odstone (now a single farm), Compton Beauchamp, Knighton, Hardwell (now a single moated farm), Woolstone and Uffington. Not all of these are or ever were parishes, merely being manors, but their presence indicates the great continuity that underlies the history of these hills.

The hills were mostly farmed in common in the Middle Ages with each villager having strips in the open fields and grazing and other rights on the hills. There are areas of ridge and furrow in the vales at the foot of the escarpment, the corrugation produced by medieval plough teams and always evidence of common field farming. There are good stretches of ridge and furrow on Walk 7, for example, down in the vale. The villages on the dip slope in the Chilterns in particular did not pursue the Midland open field system of the vales and had smaller common fields and more private hedged fields and woodland, which resulted in very different countryside. The enclosure of the open fields took place mainly in the 18th Century and early 19th Century, for example Ashbury in 1772 (Walk 6) and Monks Risborough in 1830 (Walk 22). These radical changes were usually made by individual Acts of Parliament for they in effect turned small farmers into landless labourers, robbing them of their arable strips and meadow hay doles and favouring the big farmers and landowners. Later enclosure took place under annual general Acts and these included parishes such as North Stoke under the 1856 Act (Walk 14).

Good corn country: Cherhill from Berwick Bassett Down

The physical effect of this was the creation of large arable farms up on the Downs with few if any hedges and very large fields, occasional beech copses and tree windbreaks, the prairie landscape so characteristic of the Berkshire and Marlborough Downs. Few farmhouses were built up on the windswept downs and a total contrast to the eastern part of the Berkshire Downs south-west of Streatley and the Chilterns, east of the Thames side villages where smaller fields with farmhouses prevailed.

Generally speaking the enclosure fields were large and rectangular or square, while older fields were more irregular, often with curving hedges in the S-plan, which reflected the way the medieval plough team started preparing to turn well in advance of the end of a strip. Another clue to older hedgerows is to count the woody species within them. A remarkably accurate dating of hedges is achieved by counting the number of species in a 100km (30m) stretch, preferably repeating the exercise a couple of times along the hedge's length. It is evident that new species colonise a hedge at the rate of approximately one every 100 years. Thus, most hedges on the walk have at least two species, normally hawthorn and blackthorn which takes the hedge back to the mid 19th Century or so. Frequently there are half a dozen species, usually including most of the following: thorn, blackthorn, hazel, maple, ash, elm and dogwood.

It adds to the pleasure of a walk down a winding lane or green lane with six or seven hedge species to estimate the date of the hedgerow, then glance into the field beside you to see a two-species hedge dividing the field on the other three sides. In some parishes along the foot of the Downs the first edition of the Ordnance Survey shows no hedges, only lanes, and the areas around the village are labelled 'East Hendred Field', 'North Stoke Field' (enclosed 1856) and 'South Stoke Field' (enclosed 1853), for example, which show that in the early 19th Century many villages along the Chilterns and the Downs still farmed in the medieval way.

West of the Thames old lanes are fewer in number than in the Chilterns where the pattern of land holding was very different with hamlets and dispersed farmsteads linked by ancient lanes, such as Hogtrough Lane (Walk 25), the lanes often with high banks surmounted by multi-species hedges. The landscape that we see on these walks is heavily modelled by man, of course who worked with the contours and soils nature provided as best he could. The chalk soils on the hills needed improvement which came with stock rearing in the medieval and more ancient systems of mixed farming and crop rotation. The animal dung was crucial in keeping the land productive,

The Chilterns in the snow

both arable and pasture and there is still extensive stock rearing on the Ridgeway's hills. Cattle and sheep are common and there are areas where pigs are reared in tin bungalows. Nowadays dung and lime is supplemented by chemical fertilisers and fallow only exists where the Common Agricultural Policy subsidises 'set aside'.

Farmers and landowners have always responded to market demand (or latterly European subsidy regimes) and the agriculture of various parts of he Chilterns have changed frequently over the years. The medieval woolcloth industry and the London mutton markets led to much of the Downland being converted to sheep runs and it is then that the classic Downland, bare grassland with occasional tree clumps came into being. Several villages on the hill tops were cleared away, leaving only their earthworks such as Upper Upham (Walk 4) behind.

The importance of sheep to the Downs can be seen in various of the walks, for example East Hendred with its medieval cloth fairs (Walk 10) and East Ilsley with its fortnightly sheep fairs while at its great annual fair up to 80,000 sheep were auctioned in a day (Walk 11). The Ridgeway itself served an important function as a sheep and cattle drove road, which avoided the heavier going of the vales as well as the dues and tolls of towns and villages through which such routes passed.

Until enclosure of the parishes, through which the Ridgeway passes, the route meandered along the tops, sheep, cattle, horses, pedlars, wayfarers and travellers seeking the driest and least rutted routes – not dissimilar to now where the impact of horses, cycles and other vehicles force the walker to the verges. Enclosure, mostly in the 18th Century, hedged in the Ridgeway, the width of the route varying from parish to parish, sometimes 30ft (9.14m) and in some parishes 50 or 60ft (15.24m or 18.29m). The wider the better for wild flowers it has to be said, but that is incidental. The hedges along much of the Ridgeway feature two to three species, which supports this 18th-Century date, but it also has to be admitted that few are stock proof now and most are distinctly unkempt. This neglect of course reflects the changes since enclosure, for they bound mostly great fields and relatively few pastures where nowadays stock proofing is provided by post and wire fences.

During the 18th Century, improved agriculture and enclosure allowed landowners to change from sheep to corn and the age of the prairie was born. The boom period was up to the repeal of the Corn Laws in 1846, after which protection for English corn growers ended. This phase led to the construction of some enormous barns for processing the corn, many of which survive, such as those in Ipsden (Walk 14) with their large number of waggon porches. In the Chiltern huge numbers of barns were built between 1750 and 1820, admittedly not as big as those at Ipsden, but this was a golden age for the farmer who had escaped from the inefficiency of the open field system and was now able to grow what he wanted how he wanted. Productivity increased greatly as a result and the vast fields of the Berkshire and Marlborough Downs developed, often with no hedges visible for miles, except along the pre-enclosure lanes that wound through the prairies.

The corn looks beautiful and golden in August in the warm sunshine, the breeze rustling the ripe ears, but there are many who prefer the small fields of the Chilterns interspersed by ancient woodland rich in bluebells, wild garlic and wood anemones from which the fields were carved, supplemented by hundreds of acres of beech woods and coppices to feed the insatiable demand from London for firewood, produced in coppices with beech and oak as standards. In the 18th Century there was, perforce, a shift away from this trade into furniture: coal became affordable further down the social scale, so the woods filled with Chiltern 'bodgers' and their pole lathes supplying rough shaped wood to the furniture makers of Wycombe, whose most noted product was the Windsor chair. Beech trees and coppice supplied the materials for this industry which thrived from the 18th to the 20th Centuries and had a profound effect on the landscape. Leafy Bucks, as the tag has it, refers only to the Chilterns and Burnham Beeches. There are still large areas of beech wood and woodland is not entirely absent from the Marlborough and Berkshire Downs. On Walk 2, for example, the route goes through West Woods, beech woods that cover hundreds of acres, but there is no denying that the Chilterns have many more wooded areas.

Transport improved in the 18th Century and the remoteness of the Chilterns and the Berkshire and Marlborough downs was reduced. Turnpike roads, such as that from Henley to Oxford, started in 1736, or that from High Wycombe to Oxford, turnpiked in 1719, led to much quicker journeys, but because of the tolls which could be taken at various points along the way, the Ridgeway Path, toll-free, increased in popularity with herdsmen driving their stock to market. When some turnpikes charged 10 old pence (4p) or even a shilling (5p) for a score of cattle to pass the turnpike gate this obviously increased costs of getting your stock to London or elsewhere, so the Ridgeway was as busy as ever.

Canals came later in the 18th Century and these cut through the Chilterns with the Grand Junction Canal reaching Tring in 1797 on its way towards Birmingham. These great trade arteries declined after the railways arrived: indeed the Great Western Railway bought the Kennett and Avon Canal in 1852 (Walk 1). The Thames, which cuts through the chalk hills via the Goring Gap, had long been a major trade route with several ports and wharves to export the produce and products from the hills: corn and firewood, for example. The railways supplanted the canals and again utilised the valley passes, so the London to Birmingham went through the Tring Gap in 1839, the Great Western and Brunel took the Great Western through the Goring Gap in the 1830s. Other railways crossed the chalk, including the valley of the River Og and the Risborough Gap in 1862. Modern roads also cut through the Chilterns and the Marlborough Downs, most notably the M40 and the M4.

The well house at Aldworth

The 20th Century has brought great changes in some ways, but in others the Ridgeway Path's hills are unchanging. The cornfields remain, but they are harvested by great machines rather than by hand held scythes or later, horse-drawn reapers. Tractors with long booms spray the young crops, giant ploughs turn the soil for seed drilling, sheep are herded by Land Rovers: the changes are enormous but the end products remain the same. There are, however, notable differences: fewer people work on the land, the collapse of hill barns that are now no longer needed, and the widespread use of contractors for harvesting. The Downs were sparsely inhabited but even more so now. You can walk all day and see only a couple of people outside the villages and hamlet.

There has been more 20th-Century development in the Chilterns, particularly around the towns such as Watlington, Tring and Wendover and even on the hills, such as Bledlow Ridge and Naphill. Commuters have played a major role in the Chilterns, in particular by building houses to accommodate them. These newcomers tend to be fiercest in conservation matters, which bodes well for the future, but on the other hand

Snow-covered Chiltern trees

they have driven up house prices so that local first-time buyers have no chance. Most development is off the hills with expanded towns like Aylesbury or Swindon. Villages and smaller towns have all grown, but the most intrusive and ever-present modern building that the Ridgeway walker has as a constant companion is the Didcot Power Station of 1972, whose cooling towers and even taller chimney can be seen in most Ridgeway walks: most dispiriting because you feel you are making no progress along the way at all.

It is commonly held by urban writers on the countryside that wild flowers have all but disappeared in the face of modern agro-industrial farming. This seems manifestly untrue for even in the most hedgeless of prairies there are wild flowers and wherever there is a decent verge the flowers are there in abundance. Butterflies too are not the rare object that doom merchants would have us believe. During my walking for this book I saw many species of butterflies: meadow browns, the much-rarer wall brown, gatekeepers, small skippers, small tortoiseshells, peacocks by the score, large and small whites, marbled whites, painted ladies, red admirals, brimstones, clouded yellows, blues, even a Duke of Burgundy fritillary. Nothing over spectacular perhaps but seen in sufficient numbers to be most encouraging and negate much that the doom merchants say.

These butterflies and other insects feed on a bewildering variety of wild flowers which are to be seen in July and August. Walk earlier in the year and you can see the *pièce de résistance* of the Chiltern beechwood: the bluebell. Carpets of intense azure blue flowers beneath beeches whose new leaves are an intensely bright and delicate green and certainly one of the finest and most moving sights in the English countryside and a particular glory of the Chilterns.

In July and August one of the most attractive groups of flowers in effect follow on from the bluebell, although in a much less dense way. These are the harebells whose delicate pale blue bell shaped downward pointing heads adorn many areas of grassland, whether Ridgeway Path verges or downland, such as Kingstone Downs near Ashdown House, and the violet blue flowered clustered bellflower and nettle leaved bell flower. Earlier in July you should see pyramid and early purple orchids in the Chilterns. Some of the most attractive and striking flowers include Chiltern gentians and yellow kidney vetch, and the delicate lesser centaury with its pinkish red flowers. None of these are large plants but I have a soft spot for the rosebay willowherb and the great willowherb, which can be seen in abundance on these walks adding a splash of bright reddish-purple to any woodland clearing, piece of waste ground or stream bank. Indian balsam and orange balsam, the latter by the Thames and other water courses, are spectacular fast growing plants. Great mullein and dark mullein are striking while the variety of umbellifers like wild parsley, cow parsley, are legion. Giant hogweeds are everywhere.

More common and attractive wild flowers seen along the Ridgeway Path and elsewhere on the walks include yellow agrimony, cut leaved cranesbill, red campion, white campion, cowslip, ladies bedstraw, wild mignonette, buttercups of various sorts, red bartsia, knapweeds, field scabious, devil's bit scabious, ragged robin, teasel, ribbed melilot, black medick, mouse-ear hawkweed whose perfect symmetry of petals I greatly admire, vetches and birds foot trefoils. In the hedges you would expect to see black bryony, its large shiny leaves distinctive and going black by the end of August, white bryony with its ivy like leaves, dog and field roses, blackberry brambles, clematis, wild hops, sweethearts, ivies and bittersweet. Bindweeds are often under-rated and they are a constant presence, and their trumpet-like flowers vary in size dramatically from the large white hedge bindweed to the small delicate pink and white field bindweed.

One of my favourites and very much the flower of August is the beautiful blue of the meadow cranesbill, a flower that likes track junctions as much as gatekeeper butterflies do in July and early August. Another blue flower that make a splendid splash of colour is chicory. Of the small flowered plants there are many that add to the enjoyment of the walks. Marjoram and thyme, wild basil and the corn mints and spearmints on the hills, water mint by the Thames and water courses whose leaves when rubbed give off herb or mint smells are particularly enjoyable and frequent along the way. Then there are the beetroot-coloured woundwort and the splendidly-named horehound. Larger are the startling red berry clusters of the cuckoo pint, also known as lords and ladies, the hawkweeds and in the woods the splendid arrays of the pink-purple foxgloves in July and early August, countless dead nettles with white or pink flowers, the deep blue of self heal in meadows and verges, and the ubiquitous herb robert, with its delicate pink-red flowers. Mallows are common near roads and red poppies near corn. Even in the most arid sprayed cornfields the path through shows knotweeds, redshank, feverfew, small bindweeds, vetches, docks, blue field forget-me-nots and scarlet pimpernel. Thistles of various types are numerous in all habitats and provide food for countless butterflies, as does lesser burdock. At the end of August thistledown covers the plants and blow all over in veritable snow storms. Nettles, I am sorry to say, are everywhere, usually congregating around a field stile or neglected path in the vales or well off the Ridgeway Path itself, which rarely presents such leg-stinging problems and is generally well maintained.

Hedge species have already been mentioned as have some trees. Beech is of course the typical tree of the Chilterns, and is also the main tree of the Berkshire and Marlborough Downs but less numerous. Oak, ash, sycamore, horse chestnut, lime and various conifers including Arolla and Corsican pines can be seen in many locations as woodland trees and in hedges or in avenues such as the unforgettable one to Compton Beauchamp House on Walk 7 and it is rare for a wood to be single species. Ash and sycamore get everywhere, sometimes deliberately planted, sometimes self sown. Even in as homogenous a beechwood as West Woods (Walk 2) there are interlopers, both planted as with the firs and pines in blocks within the woods, and casual like the silver birches. The undergrowth varies from wood to wood, sometimes a choking mass of bramble and holly, sometimes bracken and holly, sometimes thorn and ash scrub. There used to be vast amounts of hazel and other coppices and sometimes you come across managed coppice, but it is relatively uncommon.

In the autumn the beech trees are a wonderful sight as their leaves go golden and an autumn beechwood is a most beautiful place. Distant views of Bledlow or Whiteleaf are stunning at that time of year. However, autumn means winter is close behind and many prefer the bright greens of spring as the beech leaves emerge and sun dapples the woodland floor. The photographs in this book were taken almost entirely in summer when the walks were done, but doing the walks all the year round is commended. Winter walking with the trees bare and your breath steaming is equally enjoyable once you warm up with the exertion of walking.

On the walks you would certainly expect to see a bird that when I first walked the Ridgeway countryside in the 1970s did not exist. The red kite was re-introduced in 1989 centuries after being hunted to extinction. Breeding for the first time in 1992, the kite has proved immensely successful and in the Chilterns in particular is almost common. With their beautiful colouring and 5ft wing span and soaring flight they are a splendid addition to the hills. They are unpopular with other birds though and when walking these routes I saw them driven off and mobbed by other birds: I even saw a brace of wood pigeon chasing a kite away. Certainly they are disliked by their competitor scavengers such as carrion crow, rooks and jackdaws. Buzzards are also not infrequent, particularly on the Marlborough Downs, while kestrels and sparrowhawks are seen less on the hills and more in the vales. Peregrine falcons are spreading and can occasionally be seen in the Chilterns: again a bird of rarity in the south when I was a boy.

Rose bay willow herb

The wood pigeon is a constant companion on these walks, crashing out of trees as you approach when the sensible option would be to sit tight until the walker passes. Their blundering into the air, accompanied by a fluttering descent of a few feathers, often takes you by surprise. Pheasant, grouse and partridge all do the same thing sometimes with heart-stopping effect. Rooks, carrion crow and jackdaws caw and wheel all along the routes, but smaller birds are harder to see. Wrens are common on the hills and in the vales while gold finches hunt in packs and are surprisingly common. Skylarks, linnets, blackbirds, yellowhammers and greenfinches you should see frequently but other shy birds slip into the hedges or trees, a flash of brown and no chance of identification. Green woodpeckers and jays add a splash of colour and the magpie is, as everywhere including gardens, ever present. In many of the woods game birds are reared and these add greatly to the wildlife.

On the walks alongside water, ducks, geese, swans, grebe,

A splendid bracket fungus,
Bledlow

moorhen and coots abound. In some places more exotic ducks have been introduced, such as the canal reservoirs near Tring on Walk 28 where you will see pochard, pintail, shelduck and smew as well the more usual mallard. Here there are also terns and gulls. Swallows and house martins are everywhere in July and August whether swooping low over the Kennett and Avon Canal (Walk 1) and touching the water or sitting on electricity wires or swooping high over fields.

The most frequently seen animal on the walks is, not surprisingly, the rabbit and there are plenty of them. Walkers stand more chance of encounters with rabbits and other mammals than the more noisy user of the Ridgeway and with luck you will have an eyeball to eyeball encounter with a muntjak deer who will stand stock still and look before loping off into the thicker wood. Sika deer can also be spotted and occasional groups of fallow or roe. These all originate from escapees from such places as Stonor Park in Oxfordshire or Woburn Park in Bedfordshire and feral populations are spreading rapidly to add to the variety in the hills and woods, possibly to the chagrin of tree planters. Foxes and hare are sometimes seen going about their business and the occasional weasel will scuttle across the path. Dead voles and mice are as near as you will get to these tiny rodents, along with the odd run over badger in the lanes, supplemented by numerous flattened hedgehogs.

This sketch of what can be seen on the Ridgeway and in these walks I hope gives a flavour of the astonishing variety and richness and, I think, a tribute to the landowners and their stewardship. I frequently passed new tree plantings, usually of mixed deciduous trees, new hedges of traditional mixed species like holly, thorn, hazel, maple and blackthorn. The wild flower population seems good and it should re-assure doom merchants about the state of the countryside. Even the most intensive farms I saw had conservation areas of new planting, unmown verges and corners of fields. The fact that many hedges are neglected in a sense helps wildlife so I was most encourages by what I saw.

Down in the vales there are pockets of farms where the needs of the walker are ignored and positively hindered. Overgrown footpaths, broken stiles, nettle hidden stiles, no adequate gap between the crops and the hedge nettles: the usual sort of thing, but none are insuperable and where they are I have changed the route onto alternative public rights of way. If you do find blocked paths, please report them to the appropriate highway authority. The Rambler's Association can help you do this – see inside front cover of this book.

The walks are all circular, some start and finish in Ridgeway Path car parks, but I re-jigged several to avoid this. I know the car parks need to be used but when I did Walk 30 the Pitstone Hill car park had neat rows of shattered car window glass marking out each car parking bay from a raid by thieves the previous weekend. Some are safe, of course, and I have used them myself without incident, but there are warning signs at most of them. The other issue is that these car parks are not accessible by public transport and I have therefore taken care to ensure that most of the walks are on bus routes. The frequency of buses is an issue you will have to check for yourself, but I was particularly impressed with the Ridgeway Explorer initiative, a bus service normally running from April to the end of October on Sundays and Bank Holidays, specifically to help users of the Ridgeway Path.

Unlike other volumes in this series, there is little safety advice needed. I have never needed a compass and provided you take water or a drink and a snack or a picnic that is all you need. Normal weather precautions are necessary for English weather, but I think these walks are fundamentally safe. The climbing and descents are gentle, compared with, say, Cader Idris, the navigation relatively straightforward: map excerpts are provided for each walk, but the appropriate OS or Harvey Route Map, *Ridgeway*, should also be carried and details of these are given at the beginning of each walk.

On most of the walks there are pubs at intervals or village stores, but where there is nothing I have indicated that. The walks vary in length and some can be done in a long morning

A red admiral on lesser burdock

or afternoon, others are full-scale day walks, but all are circular so there is no car shuffling or timetable co-ordinating needed. I have enjoyed re-walking the Ridgeway Path country immensely and hope you enjoy it as much as I have. I think the walks give great variety and cover all aspects of the countryside on and around the Ridgeway Path, the constant reference point and an element in every walk.

The Chilterns, the Berkshire Downs and the Marlborough Downs contain beautiful countryside that can cater for all tastes, but the book also takes you down into the vales below the escarpment and onto the chalk plateau behind the Ridgeway Path and routes include canal towpaths, the banks of the River Thames and lake sides. Rather like the Peak District there is a huge population catchment within easy reach of the Ridgeway Path and the path is well used. Even so you meet remarkably few walkers and off the main path, as the bulk of these routes are, you will meet even fewer. There are hotspots like Avebury (Walk 3) or the Bridgewater Monument Whiteleaf (Walk 29) but few there are walkers. So despite the proximity of large populations you can savour the countryside in relative peace, although it has to be said the Ridgeway west of Goring is subject to modern mechanised leisure: trail bikes, quadbikes (these are the most unpleasant) and four-wheel drive vehicles. Mountain bikes are also common, but that said, if you avoid weekends they are not a problem. I hope you find these walks as stimulating and enjoyable to walk as I did.

How to use this book

This book contains route maps and descriptions for 30 walks. Each walk is graded (see p.3 and below) and areas of interest are indicated by symbols (see below). For each walk particular points of interest are denoted by a capital letter both in the text and on the map (where the letter appears in a red box). In the text the route descriptions are prefixed by lower-case letters. We recommend that you read the whole description, including the tinted box at the start of each walk, before setting out.

Key to maps

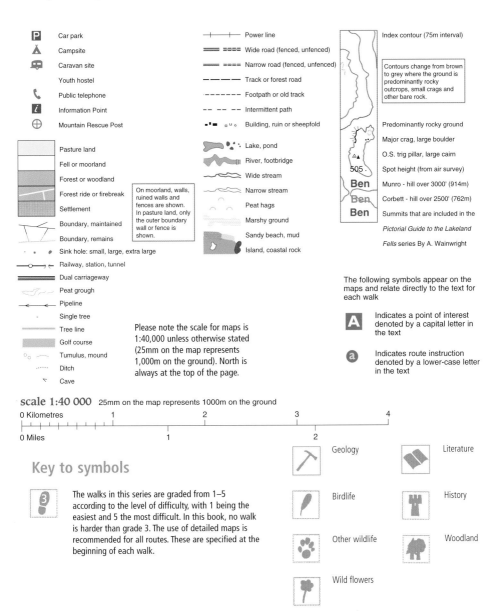

P	Car park
Ă	Campsite
	Caravan site
	Youth hostel
☎	Public telephone
i	Information Point
⊕	Mountain Rescue Post
	Pasture land
	Fell or moorland
	Forest or woodland
	Forest ride or firebreak
	Settlement
	Boundary, maintained
	Boundary, remains
	Sink hole: small, large, extra large
	Railway, station, tunnel
	Dual carriageway
	Peat grough
	Pipeline
	Single tree
	Tree line
	Golf course
	Tumulus, mound
	Ditch
	Cave

┼──┼──	Power line
	Wide road (fenced, unfenced)
	Narrow road (fenced, unfenced)
─ ─ ─ ─	Track or forest road
─ ─ ─ ─	Footpath or old track
── ── ──	Intermittent path
	Building, ruin or sheepfold
	Lake, pond
	River, footbridge
	Wide stream
	Narrow stream
	Peat hags
	Marshy ground
	Sandy beach, mud
	Island, coastal rock

On moorland, walls, ruined walls and fences are shown. In pasture land, only the outer boundary wall or fence is shown.

	Index contour (75m interval)

Contours change from brown to grey where the ground is predominantly rocky outcrops, small crags and other bare rock.

	Predominantly rocky ground
	Major crag, large boulder
Δ▲	O.S. trig pillar, large cairn
505 ·	Spot height (from air survey)
Ben	Munro - hill over 3000' (914m)
Ben	Corbett - hill over 2500' (762m)
Ben	Summits that are included in the *Pictorial Guide to the Lakeland Fells* series By A. Wainwright

The following symbols appear on the maps and relate directly to the text for each walk

A Indicates a point of interest denoted by a capital letter in the text

a Indicates route instruction denoted by a lower-case letter in the text

Please note the scale for maps is 1:40,000 unless otherwise stated (25mm on the map represents 1,000m on the ground). North is always at the top of the page.

scale 1:40 000 25mm on the map represents 1000m on the ground

0 Kilometres   1   2   3   4

0 Miles   1   2

Key to symbols

3 The walks in this series are graded from 1–5 according to the level of difficulty, with 1 being the easiest and 5 the most difficult. In this book, no walk is harder than grade 3. The use of detailed maps is recommended for all routes. These are specified at the beginning of each walk.

Geology

Literature

Birdlife

History

Other wildlife

Woodland

Wild flowers

WEST KENNETT

Those first walk is the longest in the book and packed with historic interest spanning over 5,000 years of Britain's history. It also follows the Ridgeway south from the end of the official, long-distance path for a further four spectacular miles (6.4km), before descending from the chalk escarpment to a row of fine villages along the Kennett and Avon Canal. Returning north over the hills, you reach the highest point above sea level in any of the 30 walks. Back in the River Kennett's valley the walk concludes with two of the finest Neolithic monuments in an area rich in prehistory: Silbury Hill and the West Kennett Long Barrow.

MAP:
OS Landranger Sheet 173, OS Explorer No 157 Marlborough & Savernake Forest

START/FINISH:
Layby on A4 opposite southern end of Ridgeway Path, Overton Hill, ½ mile (1km) east of West Kennett, Wiltshire SU118680. The 48, 48A and 49 buses from Swindon, some of which go on to Marlborough and Hungerford, serve West Kennett near the start of the walk. As Swindon and Hungerford have railway stations it is feasible to combine rail with buses to get to West Kennett, the start of the Ridgeway Path

DISTANCE:
17 miles (27km)

APPROXIMATE TIME:
7 hours

HIGHEST POINT:
965ft (294m) on Tan Hill SU082647

REFRESHMENTS:
On the canal, there is the Barge Inn at Honeystreet. In All Cannings there is the Kings Arms and across the Downs, the Waggon and Horses, Beckhampton

ADVICE:
The longest walk in the book and will take all day. If hot, take water and a snack, but the navigation is straightforward

Knap Hill Neolithic causeway camp

A For the Sanctuary at the start of the walk see Walk 2. East Kennett is a small attractive village on the south side of the young River Kennett. The route passes two sides of the Manor House which is a good, late Georgian brick house behind a boundary wall built of sarsen stone. Christ Church dates from 1864 and its felicitous stone broach spire can be seen rising above the trees in many distant views of the village.

a From the layby starting point, head south crossing the road and following the byway to the left of the Sanctuary. Descend past a tumulus to follow the track round to a bridleway sign and turn right to cross the River Kennett, here little more than a stream. The track becomes a lane and passes the entrance gates to the Manor House with an octagonal dovecote in the field beyond. Past a junction go right onto a footpath alongside the Manor House's stone boundary wall. At the road turn right, then left to the church. The village has many stone cottages with thatched roofs and an old school of 1857. Retrace your steps along the church lane, turn right, carry on along the road out of the village and at a junction carry on round, signposted 'Woodborough'.

The road leaves the village past thatched cottages and, on the left, a sarsen stone garden, soon bearing right onto a byway that leads past East Kennett Manor Farm. This is the Ridgeway. After 300m (990ft) you come to three gates. Pass through the one on the left to follow a grassy track to the left of a more obvious track through the valley bottom. The track now climbs steadily along the edge of a good dry valley. Peacock butterflies are plentiful throughout the walk in summer, when you may also find painted ladies feeding on the clover flowers, meadow browns, gatekeepers, whites and ringlets. The track leaves the dry valley edge and goes left into a muddy track in an oak wood with coppiced hazel and speckled woods flying. The wood thins to a belt alongside the track of hazel, oak and ash with red campion and herb robert in the verge and a parish boundary. Soon the track crosses that great linear earthwork, Wansdyke, with its deep ditch and a high bank on its south side although it is partially hidden by trees and shrubs.

Keep straight on after emerging from the woods with long views south now you have crossed the ridge. There is Knap Hill hillfort with the banks of ancient field systems and strip lynchets (low banks, which mark the outlines of the fields) on the grassy slopes to its left and Adam's Grave on the right. The path descends towards a road and just before it goes over a stile to pick up the path to Adam's Grave on its grassy knoll. From its

The Alton Barnes White Horse cut in 1812

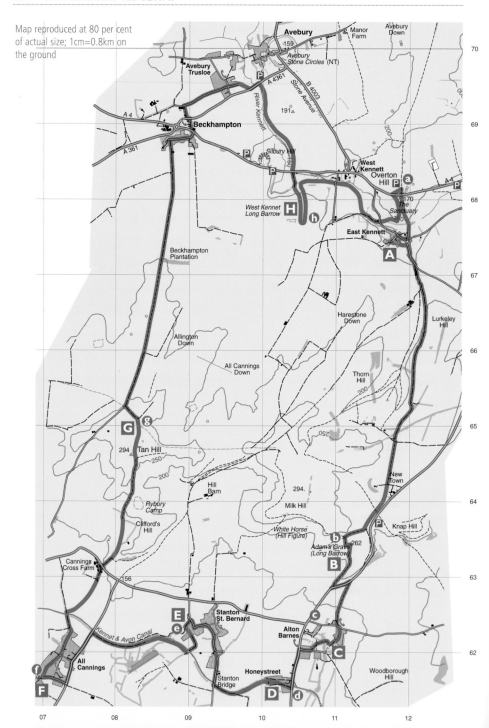

Map reproduced at 80 per cent
of actual size; 1cm=0.8km on
the ground

262m (860ft) summit look across to Knap Hill on the other side of the dry valley and enjoy the wonderful views east and west along the chalk escarpment, as well as south for many miles.

B Adam's Grave on its hill, an outlier from Walkers Hill, is a large Neolithic chambered long barrow, referred to in an Anglo-Saxon charter of AD 825 as 'Woden's Barrow', while Knap Hill, at the end of a spur from the downs, has its crest encircled by the ramparts of a Neolithic causewayed camp, which has been carbon dated to around 2750 BC.

St Mary's Church, Alton Barnes

b A pair of wall-brown butterflies danced on the summit of Adam's Grave hill when I was there. From the summit descend to the path that heads south along the ridge towards Alton Barnes, dropping over 300ft (91m) in a short distance. You will see field gentians, harebells, clustered bellflowers and felwort as the grass is rich in wild flowers. Looking right along the valley floor in the summer, a tide of colour from the crops washes up to the grassed scarp as far as the eye can see. At the point where the path reaches the road via a field gate, turn left back up the hill. After 250m (820ft) leave the road on the right and rejoin the Ridgeway at a sharp angle to head south, the path here being enclosed by trees on both sides. Cross the road and follow the lane, almost opposite, through the village to Alton Priors Church, entering the churchyard on a sarsen stone sett path.

C The two parish churches of Alton Priors and Alton Barnes are separated by a field and are both ancient churches, the latter having an Anglo-Saxon nave and the former a part Norman nave. Both have brick chancels and both churchyards have enormous and ancient yew trees. Alton Priors' 15th Century tower has a vast sundial and Alton Barnes has a monument of 1590, which should not be missed by connoisseurs of the absurd. West of Alton Barnes church the old rectory is a fine Georgian house of about 1730.

c Out of the church follow the sett path west and cross streams on bridges, then diagonally left, still on setts to Alton Barnes church. From the church walk along the lane, a sycamore avenue, to the junction, passing the old rectory on the right. Turn left along the road and head south to Honeystreet.

D Honeystreet Wharf, built in 1811, was a depot on the Kennett and Avon Canal. A tall chimney from one of the industrial buildings on the site survives, as do several of the

Wansdyke looking west

buildings and the canalside cottages. At the west end is the Barge Inn, a most welcome stop for a drink. The Kennett and Avon was completed in 1810 and linked the west country to London via the Thames. It was a great success but fell into decline after its rival, the Great Western Railway, bought it in 1852.

d At Honeystreet turn right onto the canal towpath and, passing the Barge Inn, leave at the next bridge, No 125, and turn right to walk into Stanton St Bernard, passing on the right the Manor House. Past a telephone kiosk go left along a path behind 1860s estate cottages to the church.

E Stanton St Bernard's Manor House is built in sarsen stone with limestone dressings which include the excellent arched doorway and 1677 date plaque. All Saints church was rebuilt in 1832, apart from the pleasing 15th-Century west tower.

e Leave the church via a cobble path amid horse chestnuts and limes, through bollards and turn left through Church Farm, right past the Pewsey Vale Riding Centre, then left through a gate onto a metalled track which soon bears right to England's Bridge over the canal, passing a World War II pillbox with a wide aperture for an artillery piece.

Over the canal bridge rejoin the towpath to continue westward to All Cannings Bridge, No 127. Along the canal bank are great willowherb, reeds, teasels, downy thistles, melilot, storksbill and betony, while house martins swooped for insects, splashing and rippling the canal surface. There were several dragonflies darting along the bank and in the canal moorhen and their young. Leave the canal at Bridge No 127 and turn left to walk along the road, turning right just past the gates to The Grange, signposted 'All Cannings'. Turn left into the Glebe, an estate of modern houses, and follow the road round and take the path next to No 31 to cross a paddock diagonally right, then left between gardens to emerge beside old brick farm buildings and opposite the recreation ground. Turn right and head for the church.

F　All Saints, All Cannings, is a large cruciform church with a heavy central tower, mainly 15th Century but with a fine south chapel and transept of 1508 and a spectacular High Victorian chancel of 1867. Inside, the Ernele monument of 1581 is an ornate piece with flanking pilasters and a cornice crowned by three eagles, but the most noticeable feature is that every letter 'n' is back to front.

f　From the church walk north, turning left to the Kings Arms for lunch or a drink, before continuing north past the post office stores. There are many good buildings in the village and several timber-framed and thatched houses with ogee braces, including Rustic Farm. Follow the lane out of the village to cross the canal at Woodway Bridge, Bridge No 128. Immediately over the bridge, bear right off the track into fields and head diagonally to Cannings Cross Farm where the barns are now converted to houses. Straight over the road onto a bridleway climb to a gate with agrimony and meadow cranesbill in the verge. Go through the left gate onto a bridleway along the edge of the field, then across a dry valley through crops to a stile. Over this, in sheep pasture, the path climbs the flanks of Clifford's Hill, surmounted by Rybury, a Neolithic causeway camp partly overlaid by an Iron Age hillfort which seems never to have been completed. From this climb diagonally left up the steep side of the valley to the summit beyond a stile, at 965ft (294m) the highest point in the book. The track then descends to cross Wansdyke, here a splendid ditch with high banks on each side which stretches away west and east, a spectacular feature in the landscape.

G　Like Grim's Dyke, Wansdyke, a corruption of Woden's Dyke, is attributed to Anglo-Saxon gods. In fact it was probably a boundary between two groups of Anglo-Saxon settlers as their conquests swept westward, possibly dug by the Wiltshire Saxons in the 6th Century AD. The eastern section is over 14 miles long and west of the Ridgeway is truly vast.

g Through Wansdyke turn left along a metalled track, then right at a junction, pausing to look west along Wansdyke below stretching away into the distance. Head north, mostly on a track, to reach the road at Beckhampton, turning right to walk through the village, then up steps to the main road with the Waggon and Horses pub opposite.

Across the main road, the A4, a bridleway sign, the path passes up the left hand side of the pub car park, then alongside cottage gardens and over the A4361 onto a lane with two Standing Stones ahead, large sarsens (there were three at one time). Right at the junction the lane passes through Avebury Trusloe, with older cottages, mostly built in sarsen stone, on this lane with modern development to the north. Over the crossroads descend past more cottages, one thatched, and over a stile to the right to cross the field diagonally left to a stile. Walk along the left verge of the main road and cross the road onto the bridleway signed West Kennett Long Barrow. At this point you are very close to the main car park at Avebury. The path follows the stream south to the A4 with the enormous and mysterious flat topped hill of Silbury Hill on the right. Astonishingly this hill completed by about 2300 BC, over 125ft high and tapering from 550ft at the base to a 100ft-wide flat top, is man-made.

The interior of West Kennett Long Barrow

Over the road, go through a kissing gate and follow the track across a cress bedded stream, the River Kennett in its infancy, through a kissing gate and left, then right to ascend the hill between post and wire fences to West Kennett Long Barrow.

H This long barrow burial mound was built around 3500 BC and has burial chambers off a central passage into which you can walk. It was last used around 2200 BC. The barrow is indeed long: 340ft (104m) with a row of standing sarsens as a kind of facade. This is far more impressive than Wayland's Smithy (Walk 6) and actually to walk into a Neolithic building, albeit a tomb, is quite an experience.

h Descend back to the White Horse Trail and turn right to continue east, parallel to the stream bank, cross a lane and continue, curving right and the path becomes a green lane. At the next junction, turn left along a track to another lane, turn left then right onto a bridleway, along the north side of the stream. Through a hedge, turn left onto the track back up to the A4 at Overton Hill and the southern end of the Ridgeway Path and of this walk.

WEST OVERTON AND FYFIELD

As with the first walk in the book this route starts at the end of the official end of the Ridgeway Path and explores the countryside to the south east of the Ridgeway, firstly the delightful wooded hills through which the Wansdyke linear earthwork runs and then the villages along the Kennett valley west of Marlborough.

A Immediately south-west of the start, across the A4, is the Sanctuary. This Neolithic site is at the end of the ceremonial sarsen stone Avenue linking the site to the Avebury stone circle. The Sanctuary had several building periods and excavations revealed two concentric stone circles and four

MAP:
OS Landranger Sheet 173, OS Explorer No 157 Marlborough & Savernake Forest

START/FINISH:
Car Park at end of Ridgeway Path, Overton Hill, Wiltshire SU11868. The 48, 48A and 49 buses from Swindon, some of which go on to Marlborough and Hungerford, serve West Kennett near the start of the walk. As Swindon and Hungerdord have railway stations it is feasible to combine rail with buses to get to the start of the Ridgeway Path

DISTANCE:
8½ miles (13.5km)

APPROXIMATE TIME:
4 hours

HIGHEST POINT:
711ft (217m) at Strawberry Ground in West Woods SU151655

REFRESHMENTS:
The only pub on the route is the quaintly named 'The Who'd A Thought It' in Lockeridge. There is also a village shop in West Overton, the Overton Stores

ADVICE:
There is an element of road in this walk but there are no busy stretches

Tumulus at West Overton at the start of the walk

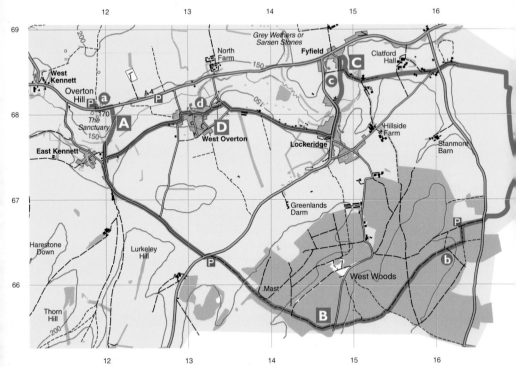

Map reproduced at 90 per cent of actual size; 1 cm = 0.9 km on the ground

timber post circles. About 2000 BC the last phase stone circle was built, at the same time as was the Avenue. The site is relatively flat and the stone circles survived until 1724, when they were removed so the farmer could plough his hill top. The posts and the socket holes, excavated in 1930, are now marked by concrete posts which must puzzle the sheep who graze the monument's field.

a The route initially is the same as that in Walk 1, crossing the road from the start of the Ridgeway Path, visiting the Sanctuary, and heading south down the byway, passing a tumulus or burial mound to the left. The path curves left and at a byway sign go right to cross the Kennett, continue along a lane shaded by tall horse chestnuts and limes on the left and the sarsen stone wall to East Kennett Manor House on the right. Ignore a left turn and at a junction by a thatched cottage turn left, signposted 'Woodborough', to follow the road past a row of thatched cottages and out of East Kennett village, past a sarsen stone 'garden' on the left.

There is a grass track parallel to the road which, although not a public right of way, can be used to avoid walking on the road, a hedgeless gentle climb between fields. Cross the junction to West Overton and continue uphill, passing the site of Hill Barn, whose sheltering stand of beech and ash trees survive. Hedges now appear including thorn, blackthorn, elder, dogwood and maple with ivy, dog roses, black bryony and sweethearts covering them. The road descends to the valley bottom and at the junction, accompanied usually by meadow cranesbills, where you turn left, then quickly right onto a metalled track between post and wire fences, choked by nettles, thistles and hogweed in summer, to climb towards the woods and a cellular phone mast. The green lane winds uphill with clouds of craneflies in the grass and rooks cawing and pigeons cooing from the woods ahead.

Follow the track into the beechwood, ignoring the bridleway off to the left, to walk amid tall trunked beeches. The track descends to the valley floor and climbs straight out, past another bridleway off to the left. Speckled woods feed on the blackberries in a clearing, bracken and brambles become more common. The track bears left and Wansdyke converges from the right. Across a track the path climbs with Wansdyke on the right, a hazel coppiced rampart and bracken filled ditch. Ignore another left turn bridleway and carry on along the track with fields beyond Wansdyke and, in the summer, woundwort, red campion, yellow vetch, ragwort, herb robert and buttercups alongside.

Wansdyke in West Woods

Where the track turns right go straight on between post and rail barriers past a post with a yellow arrow. Continue on the bridleway, ignoring the footpath sign pointing left to follow the path alongside Grimsdyke. At a path crossroads go left, then right, to follow the yellow arrows painted on trees along the other side of Wansdyke, the dyke choked with bracken and bramble and nowhere near as impressive as the stretch on the open downs in Walk 1.

B Wansdyke runs east across the Marlborough Downs roughly from the Roman settlement of Verlucio near Bromham at the end of a long straight westward stretch of a Roman road, continues past Marlborough almost to the edge of the Savernake Forest. This fact probably supports the boundary marker theory. The Roman road would be an obvious boundary in the immediate post-Roman occupation landscape as the Saxon armies moved west in the 5th and 6th Centuries, dividing territory as they went. The route follows the dyke for a mile and a half entirely within woodland until it turns south-eastward near Daffy Copse.

b   Where the dyke goes right the path carries straight on, now surfaced for wheelchairs. At a cross track go straight over and, at the next cross track a hundred yards on, turn left to emerge from the woods at a lane by a four-way bridleway signpost. Turn right onto the lane and at the road junction where a sign on the right welcomes you to the Forestry Commission's West Woods, cross to a stile and ascend cow pasture steeply and diagonally left to the hedgeline along the crest. A beautiful, dry valley with steep pasture on this side and woodland on the west slopes curves gently north-west into the Kennett Valley.

At the crest, follow the thick thorn and blackthorn hedge northwards to a stile, now on the White Horse Trail. In the next field thorn scrub is invading the slopes and where blackthorn scrub is advancing near a somewhat decrepit downhill hedge, follow the path right into the scrub and over a stile into a field beyond the hedge. Head across a set-aside field diagonally left to the end of a tree line, in fact the edge of the cleared north-half of Manton Copse, with masses of scarlet pimpernel and field forget-me-nots underfoot in Spring, as well as the detritus of clay pigeons. At the top leave the White Horse Trail, going left onto a grassy track between fields descending towards a wood, with good long views over as far as Cherhill with its Lansdowne Obelisk. The path goes right of the woods over a stile full of nettles in the corner, cross a track and out over a

St Nicholas' Church, Fyfield

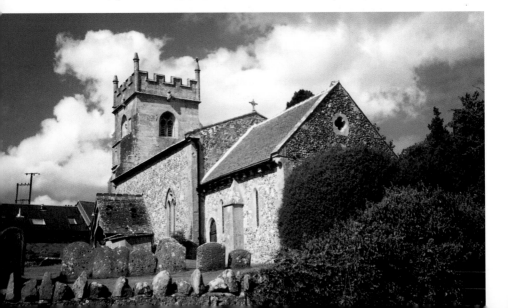

stile, also nettle-choked, to follow the hedge to a gate. Beside the gate is a stile. Over this and over another, follow the edge of the field west and north to a stile. On the day I walked here there were some superb clouded yellows, darting around the hedge edges, feeding on field scabious and flitting across the field. All were fairly orange examples and a delight to see. To the right you can see the spirelet and tower from Marlborough College's Chapel, built in the 1880s, on the skyline.

Over the stile, turn left onto a lane to follow the contour line above the Kennett Valley with meadow cranesbill, bindweed, hawkweed and vetch in the verges. Straight over a crossroads and at a bend take the right fork onto a metalled lane, opposite a cottage built in rat-trap brick bond, that is an economical use of bricks laid on edge. Past some cottages, Long Cottage and Harlaw, the route follows a well-marked grass track between horse paddocks with a view of the rear elevation of the 16th-Century Clatford Hall, stone and many-gabled, with some mullioned and transomed windows. Along the edge of a field and through a gate and past a cottage with a thatched boundary wall, the route reaches a lane. Turn right over a bridge across the young River Kennett, walk between hop covered hedges, then a beech hedge on the right, and follow the lane to Fyfield church.

Sarsen Stone gateposts near Fyfield

C   St Nicholas church, Fyfield, has a good font with the tub decorated with interlocking blind arcading. The 15th-Century tower is in fine cut ashlar stone and the tower arch into the nave has panelled reveals. The main part of the village fronts the A4, but this route goes only as far north as the church in its delightful churchyard.

c   Retrace your steps as far as Pheasants, a thatched stone cottage on the left. Leave the lane onto a footpath to the right of a Dutch barn and south through cattle pasture. Leave the fields through a gate onto the drive to a cottage. At the road turn left and re-cross the Kennett, round the bend into Lockeridge, passing the Who'd A Thought It pub. The pub and several cottages are of 1880s vernacular style with timber-framed style upper storeys and sarsen stone bands in the brickwork. Past the 1874 school, also with sarsen stone band courses, turn right, signposted 'West Overton', and follow the lane shaded by mature horse chestnuts, limes, beeches, ashes, oaks and sycamores, climbing gently. Over the brow the lane descends. Turn right at a bench installed for enjoyment of the view over the village and descend a lane over-arched by lime, beech, thorn and ash trees to the church.

D St Michael's church, West Overton, is entirely Victorian, being rebuilt in 1878. It has an impressive tower that can be seen to good effect in long views and has a large sundial inscribed: 'Watch and Pray, Time Steals Away'. The village is a long one with a mix of thatched cottages and newer ones.

d Out through the west side of the churchyard descend to the lane with shrunken village earthworks in the paddock on the left. Keep along the road, passing the Overton Stores and going left, then right, ignoring a left turn to walk along the lane to East Kennett between high hedges with spindle as well as thorn, blackthorn, maple, elder and hazel. At the T-junction, turn right to follow the lane back across the Kennett and then continue along the track west and north, back to the start of the Ridgeway Path.

The young River Kennet at Lockeridge

THE AVEBURY STONE CIRCLES AND GREY WETHERS ON THE DOWNS

This walk starts in one of the most remarkable ancient monuments in England and more impressive in its way than Stonehenge: the Avebury Stone Circles. From here the route heads east to the sarsen fields on Overton Down before descending from the Ridgeway to follow a winter bourne, that is a stream often dry in summer, through a string of charming villages back to Avebury. It can be very wet underfoot in winter.

A The Avebury Stone Circles is quite the most exciting prehistoric monument in England: no question. A circular bank and ditch surround about 28 acres, an area big enough for the High Street and Green Street of Avebury village to occupy a small part, while modern main roads utilise the original entrances to the circle. When built, the top of the rampart was about 55ft (16.8m) above the bottom of the ditch. Within was a circle of 100 standing sarsen stones, most of which survive in the two western quadrants. In the centre were two further smaller circles of stones, some of which remain, but in the 18th Century many were broken up and used to build houses in the village. A stone avenue ran from Avebury to the Sanctuary, further circles near the start of the Ridgeway (Walks 1 & 2). This is a fascinating part of the country, dotted with enigmatic remnants of our Neolithic past, but Avebury also has more modern buildings of quality including the Elizabethan manor house and gardens, parts of which are open to visitors, as well as a fine, thatched barn whose aisles date to the 17th Century, and St James' church. This was quite deliberately located outside the pagan circle and is a most rewarding one with an Anglo-Saxon nave, Norman aisles and font. From the outside the church looks mostly 15th Century with its tall, elegant tower and battlemented aisles.

a From Avebury car park, follow the signs to the village and the stone circle. After doing justice to Avebury, head east along High Street, cross the A4361 and head down Green Street out of the village, passing through the ramparts on tarmac as far as Manor Farm's modern farmbuildings after which it becomes and unmade byway known as the Herepath, 'here' being Saxon for army. In the summer verges are restharrow, wild mignonette, toadflax and ling, among others wild flowers. The track climbs to cross the Ridgeway Path, through a gate into the Fyfield Down National Nature Reserve. An information

MAP:
HARVEY Route Map Ridgeway; OS Landranger Sheet 173, OS Explorer No 157 Marlborough & Savernake Forest

START/FINISH:
Avebury, Wiltshire. Car-park on A4361 south-west of village SU099696. Avebury is served by the 48, 48A and 49 buses from Swindon. Some go on to Marlborough and Hungerford. As Swindon and Hungerdord have railway stations it is feasible to combine rail with buses to get to Avebury from further afield

DISTANCE:
10½ miles (17km)

APPROXIMATE TIME:
5 hours

HIGHEST POINT:
886ft (270m) Ridgeway Path at Berwick Bassett Down SU124731

REFRESHMENTS:
National Trust café in Avebury Manor Barn, the Red Lion pub and Post Office Stores. An ice-cream van in the car park appears at weekends. In the villages on the west arm of the route: the White House, Winterbourne Bassett, and the New Inn. Winterbourne, Monkton

ADVICE:
Time does not allow for visiting either the Stones or the Manor in Avebury. The car park fills rapidly on summer weekends

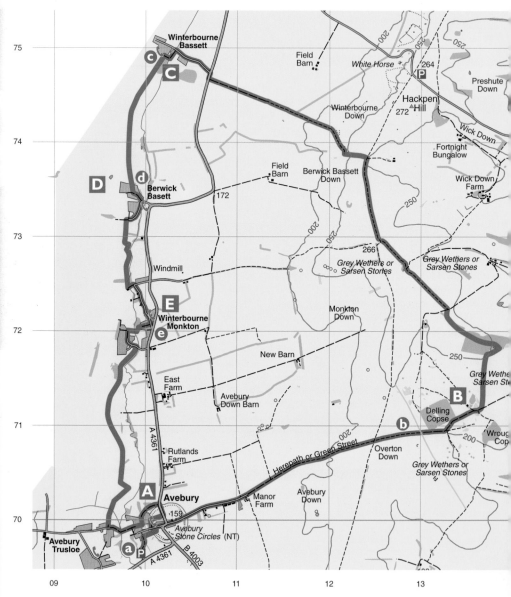

board informs you that this is one of the most important geological sites in Britain where natural events have created dry valleys with spectacular quantities of sarsen stones amid Celtic and medieval field systems. Continue straight on eastwards along a grassy path through downland pasture littered with sarsens, amid which sheep graze.

B   Sarsen stones are a natural phenomenon formed around 50 million years ago when England was sub tropical and the chalkland was covered in shallow deposits of sand and gravel. Under pressure, or due to chemical changes, the quartz sand grains fused into a fine, very hard stone which subsequent Ice Ages brought to the surface by erosion and broke up into separate blocks. Fyfield Down is a spectacular example, but sarsens are found all over the area and were used for building until recently, and indeed were ideal for Neolithic religious circles, avenues, standing stones and tombs. A similar stone in the Buckinghamshire Chilterns is known as Denner Hill Stone (Walk 26). In Wiltshire they are also known as grey wethers because of their resemblance to flocks of sheep or wethers, a wether being a castrated ram.

b   The path crosses a linear earthwork, then horserace training gallops. The path is now metalled and descends towards a beechwood, Delling Copse, through medieval ridge and furrow. Keeping on the track turn left at a fork, climb out of the dry valley amid gorse and thorn scrub and through a gate adjacent to a cottage. Soon turn left through a second gate, signed Hackpen Hill, to head diagonally northwards right across sarsen littered pasture with harebells along a grassy track, which you leave to cross to a gate by woodland. Pass through and turn right to walk alongside a post and wire fence. By a gate, turn sharp left into the woods where the path winds muddily amid hazel and ash coppice, littered with sarsens. Emerging from the wood with chicory in bright blue flower by the adjacent field opening, walk alongside hedges north-west (ensure that the pond is to your left) for about ¾ mile or 1.2km back to the Ridgeway Path which is reached via a gate.

On the Herepath east of Avebury

The Ridgeway Path here is the parish boundary of the villages in the Winterbourne valley to the west, with their upland pasture and commons. There are fine views westwards to the Cherhill

Sarsen stone on Fyfield Down

Monument. Continue on the Ridgeway Path and where it starts climbing, turn left on to a byway opposite double metal gates and a byway sign. Continue westwards on the grassy path for about 230m (750ft). The path goes through a gate, not the bridleway gate to the left of it, then right to skirt old chalkstone pits. The track soon bears left to descend the escarpment with feverfew, harebells, bedstraw, field scabious, trefoils, ling, yellow vetch, black medick and hawkweed in the verges.

The downland section of this walk is rich in butterflies: painted ladies, peacocks, red admirals, small tortoiseshells, meadow browns, gatekeepers (many actually by gates which is reassuring), red admirals, ringlets, speckled woods, small skippers, blues and of course numerous whites. The track then heads for the road with patchy wild flowers including meadow cranesbill, lesser burdock, woundwort and bittersweet. At the road turn right, then left to Winterbourne Bassett, a pub sign for the White Horse at the main road. Just before the White Horse pub turn left into a lane, signposted 'To C XIII Church'.

C St Katherine's church has some high-quality, decorated Gothic 14th-Century work, probably paid for by the then Lords of the Manor, the Despencers. The north transept was probably their family chapel and has an ornate tomb recess.

c From the church, turn right out of the porch to the gate, crossing gravel and a stile, walk through pasture to the right of the stone Victorian former rectory, then through a deer farm, the deer within high, wire-netted fields. Continue south across field, track, clapperbridge and the earthworks at the medieval village of Richardson, grazed now by cattle. Go through two gates and join an enclosed track with a plantation on the left, heading south towards Berwick Bassett. At the farmbuildings, turn left crossing a concrete road, then right to an enclosed path. At a gate, cross the stile on the right into a churchyard.

The Avebury stone circle, the north-west quadrant

D St Nicholas's church, redundant and maintained by the Churches Conservation Trust, is in a delightful location in its churchyard with the manor house to the south. The church has an 18th-Century brick chancel, but the rest, including the Victorian tower porch is built in sarsen stone: it is even used for some gravestones. The old manor house is from the 15th Century, with a stone ground floor and timber-framed upper floor: most picturesque.

St James' Church, Avebury

d Leave the churchyard through a kissing gate into an enclosed path emerging opposite the 1847 National School, now a house. Turn left to follow the road winding through the village, and passing Berwick House Farm. Continue along the road and, at a footpath sign, turn left onto a grass path with the hedge to the left. Shortly, the path turns left, still along the edge of the field, and then turns right to follow the stream, in summer a dry winter bourne. Continue straight on through a poplar spinney, to emerge onto a muddy track. At a cottage, turn left onto a lane, over the cress-choked stream bed, and turn right to follow the lane into Winterbourne Monkton.

E St Mary Magdalene's church, Winterbourne Monkton, was built by the great Victorian architect, William Butterfield in 1878, reusing parts of the medieval church such as the south porch and some traceried windows. The font is Norman with a chevron upper part above a tapering lower stage with scallops. The belfry is supported from within the nave by two huge circular posts.

e Pass the New Inn, then just before the old National School, now a house, turn right onto a narrow lane, which becomes a path that turns left, then right round cottages, crosses the stream and turns left to follow its bank before turning right. At a lane, turn left and then into the churchyard. Leave the churchyard via a kissing gate and turn right and follow the road as it curves left. Just before the stream bridge turn right through nettles and cross the stile. Now in pasture follow the stream and at the end of the field go to the right along the south hedge to a stile. Turn left over a cattle grid, and immediately right over a stile into pasture to head west to the field corner where you turn south to walk alongside a post and wire fence within cattle pasture. Continue south, crossing a lane, and crossing stiles. Avebury church tower becomes visible above the trees. Cross a stile in a thick hedge, follow the path along the hedge southwards across pasture to a stile, then, over a footbridge with stiles at each end. Over to the left are the garden walls to Avebury Manor with ball finials to the gate piers. Across the footbridge, head for a stile and, over it, turn left to walk back into Avebury.

THE OGBOURNES AND DESERTED DOWNLAND VILLAGES

MAP:
HARVEY Route Map Ridgeway;
OS Landranger Sheets 173 &
174, OS Explorer No 157
Marlborough & Savernake
Forest

START/FINISH:
Main Street, Ogbourne St
George, Wiltshire SU198743.
Ogbourne St George is served
by several bus routes between
Marlborough and Swindon,
including the Nos 70, 70A, 5,
6, and 15. As Swindon has a
railway station it is feasible to
combine rail with buses to get
to the start from further afield
by public transport

DISTANCE:
12½ miles (20km)

APPROXIMATE TIME:
4½ hours

HIGHEST POINT:
856ft (261m) Ridgeway Path
at Whitefield Hill SU212765

REFRESHMENTS:
In Ogbourne St George: The
Old Crown pub (the Inn With
the Well). Parkland Hotel and
Restaurant in Main Street. In
Ogbourne St Andrew there is
the Wheatsheaf Inn

ADVICE:
No refreshment for 10 miles,
so take water and a snack
with you, particularly if the
weather is hot. Parts of the
walk can be very muddy in
winter

AOgbourne St George is now by-passed by the A346, but architecturally is a little disappointing, although the area around the church end of the village is charming. Also unlike most villages there are working farms still within the village, such as Park Farm in Main Street. The manor is one of several in this book held by the Norman Abbey of Bec Maud of Wallingford, who granted it in around 1150, also granted several in the Wallingford area, such as North Stoke and Ipsden (Walk 14). Bec built a priory here where the present Manor House is to the west of the church but no trace now remains. The Manor House itself has a Jacobean north front with mullioned and transomed windows, dated 1619. St George's church has a 13th-Century south arcade, but from outside looks mostly 15th-Century, apart from the chancel, which is 1873 Decorated Gothic style.

a   From Main Street walk west to cross a stream, the River Og, virtually dry in August, its bed filled by cress and reeds, then right, signposted to the church, and head to the church with the stream on the right and the wall to the Manor House grounds on the left. There is a view of the Manor House from the churchyard and from the field to the north, although largely screened by lime trees. Leave the churchyard via a stile in a beech hedge from its north-west corner into a

Faithful unto death: tombs in Ogbourne St George churchyard

paddock, which gives a view back to the Manor House. Cross this diagonally to a stile behind a sycamore tree. Over this go straight on to a stile while the hedge diverges to the right, then follow post and wire fences north to a stile into a green lane, Woolmer Drove, and turn right, leaving the pastures in the valley floor behind. Walk along the lane between thorn, blackthorn, maple, elder, wych elm and hazel hedges, while in the summer, black bryony, brambles and sweethearts festoon the unkempt hedges. Across a footpath junction, the hedges are neater and wild flowers appear more numerous, including black medick, yellow vetch and meadow cranesbill.

At bridge abutments (there is no bridge deck), turn left onto the Cheseldon and Marlborough Railway Path and follow it northwards, a wide trackway between decayed thorn hedges, and positively a wild flower reserve including agrimony, wild basil, bittersweet, dog rose hips, trefoils, rosebay willowherb and St John's wort in the summertime. Peacock, speckled woods and tortoiseshells are numerous and, after crossing a lane, the path goes through a cutting, rich in ripe blackberries on the brambles. Descend to the right at a bridge abutments and turn right onto a track-cum-rubbish dump up to the main road. Turn right onto this and follow the east or far verge for about 200 noisy yards to a byway sign and turn left onto this, a tarmac lane.

Early morning haze in the Og valley

The lane climbs out of the valley steeply between thorn and blackthorn hedges, again draped in black bryony and wild roses. Liddington Castle can be seen away on the left and buzzards cruise the thermals along the scarp edge. The hedges virtually disappear at the crest and at the telecom mast the tarmac stops, and the byway becomes a green lane. At the highest point on the walk, the route reaches the Ridgeway Path and turns left onto it, a much rutted section with an alternative side path for walkers, suspiciously carved up in its turn by tyres and horses hooves. The Path descends and jinks right and left, but our route leaves it here and heads east, signed 'Byway', in effect straight on where the Ridgeway Path turns left.

The path descends across the head of a dry valley and then climbs, all silent and peaceful except for the rustling of the crops and the distant cooing of pigeons, into Upper Upham.

B   To the left beyond the row of beeches are the excellent and clear earthworks of the deserted medieval village cleared for sheep pasture to feed the cloth industry of Wiltshire and

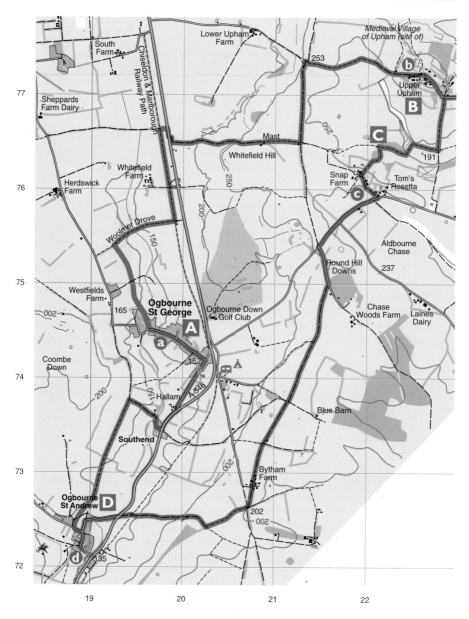

Berkshire. Further on Upham Court can be seen from the lane, a most attractive E-plan house built by Thomas Goddard in 1599 in stone with mullioned and transomed windows and stone tile roofs. Lower wings were added by the splendidly named architect Biddulph Pinchard in 1913.

b Having passed the village earthworks, with modern farmbuildings on the right, continue to a junction with a postbox on the corner. Carry straight on for sufficient distance to obtain good views of Upham Court, then retrace your steps to the postbox and turn left onto the byway, a metalled track, that descends to the bottom of a dry valley where the route turns right at a footpath sign on a low post with a hedge on the left. Where the hedge bears right carry straight on through the hedge and turn left, an old wind pump on the right, and keep on the hedged green lane. Where it turns right there is a stone plaque 'In Memory of the People of Snap, Toothill School 5–8–1991'. Ignore a footpath sign to the left 'Woodend' and climb uphill with an ash and sycamore copse on the right shielding the view of Snap deserted village earthworks. Just before a gate into the village site the green lane turns left at a byway sign to climb in a pretty holloway along the edge of a hazel coppice. Leaving the coppice behind it becomes a level green lane and then passes through the farmyard of Snap Farm to turn left into a lane past farm cottages.

Upham Court

C Snap village had been in decline for many years but is a rare example of a village finally deserted in the 20th Century without reservoir building being involved.. The last 15 houses or so were destroyed in 1913 and vocal criticism of this was countered with a suit for slander. The plaque we saw earlier is a poignant commemoration of the village.

c Continue along the lane and at the main road turn right to follow it, walking on the verges, across a dry valley, passing Cheldene, a cat-breeding and boarding establishment and considerably quieter than any canine equivalent passed on these walks. Keep on the road until reaching the Ridgeway Path to turn left, the path here following a lane. The Path bears right off the lane and becomes a metalled track. Follow it until at a track crossroads the Ridgeway Path turns right to descend towards Ogbourne St George.

The route carries straight on along a metalled track. Holsteiner cattle graze in the fields on the edge of the valley side on the

The lime avenue leading to the porch at Ogbourne St Andrew's church

right and the track passes through Bytham Farm, then across a lane, becoming a grassy path with an iron park fence on the right and post and wire on the left with many oaks and thorns. The path curves right to cross a metalled track into a hazel, ash and maple shaded byway. In a summer clearing, commas, blues, speckled woods and white butterflies feast on a mass of spearmint. Beyond the path becomes very nettly and brambly in summer. Emerging at a track, turn right onto a grassy track to descend the valley scarp, a rich variety of wild flowers amid the verges and on the banks include wild mignonette, ragged robin, clustered bellflowers, harebells and bedstraws while butterflies seem wonderfully numerous, particularly peacocks, skippers and blues. At the bottom of the scarp the track crosses the old railway line to the main road. Crossing this, continue down the lane towards Ogbourne St Andrew with the dry bed of the River Og alongside, clearly a winter bourne rather than a regular river living up to its name. Over a bridge continue following the road left into the village as far as the main road where beyond the war memorial is the Wheatsheaf Inn.

D St Andrew's church, Ogbourne St Andrew, approached by an attractively pruned lime avenue, has a part Norman nave and a good 15th-Century tower in fine cut ashlar, while the rest of the church is flint with limestone dressings. The village has some good cottages, some timber-framed and thatched, such as The Forge, and others built in sarsen stone also thatched, while there are some more formal Georgian farmhouses and an old rectory, now Tresco House, of 1848 by William Butterfield.

d From the Wheatsheaf walk back through the village, turning left into Church Lane and the churchyard. After visiting the church leave from the north end of the churchyard, over a lane and through a paddock to a gate. Through this turn right and immediately left to follow a track northward with toadflax and meadow cranesbill in the summer verges. It crosses the thick hedged parish boundary between the two Ogbournes, and after another stretch meets the Ridgeway Path descending from Coombe Down. Turn right to follow it to descend to the hamlet of Southend, which has some genuine old cottages, mostly thatched, and a couple of new, also thatched. At the main road turn left to walk along the pavement to Ogbourne St George, the main road soon bearing right to by pass the village. Straight on walk through the village and, if wished, visit the Old Crown before turning left into Main Street.

LIDDINGTON CASTLE AND BISHOPSTONE

This walk follows a line of villages built on the springline, where the chalk of the Downs ends and the greensand begins, still above the flat lands of the Vale so the villages are hilly and some have deep cut valleys with streams. From Bishopstone the route climbs up onto the chalk Downs, then south and west to Liddington Castle, the highest point on the Ridgeway and where the hills turn eastward into Oxfordshire. The route then descends to the spring line villages back to Bishopstone.

A Bishopstone, near the Oxfordshire border, has lanes focused on a stream that emerges a little south of the village and winds through it in a steep, little valley, part dammed for a mill pond. South of the main through road the whitewashed thatched cottages climb the valley sides, linked by narrow alleys and paths. All quite delightful, while the church is in the northern part of the village, between two streams. St Mary has an ornate reset Norman doorway but the rest is generally from the 15th Century. South of the main road by the mill pond, the school of 1849 is built in fine cut chalk stone.

a Beside the school, pass along a footpath opposite Cues Lane to wind between gardens and thatched cottages. Past Finch Hill Cottage, turn sharp left to climb steeply to the road, turning right into Nell Hill. Just before the de-restriction sign, at a footpath sign bear right onto a metalled track which descends past more thatched cottages and becomes a path with Indian balsam flowers alongside in the summer. Through a kissing gate there were strip linchets visible on both sides of the flat-bottomed valley. Over a stile, walk to the left, up the sheep-cropped valley, gradually climbing. Through a gate the valley curves right, narrows and widens up to the Ridgeway Path.

Cross the Ridgeway Path onto a metalled track, signed 'bridleway', with meadow cranesbill on the verges near the junction. The track climbs steadily to skirt Lammy Down, mostly between fields. There are views of Uffington Castle and Ashdown Park to the left before the track goes through a field and, as post and wire fences re-appear, descends a dry valley with crops on the right and pasture on the left. The pasture is rich in wild summer flowers including spiny restharrow and mouse ear hawkweed. After a mile or so the track emerges from the valley through a gate and follows the metalled track to the road. Turn

MAP:
OS Landranger Sheet 174, OS Explorer No 157 Marlborough & Savernake Forest, No 170 Abingdon, Wantage & Vale of White Horse

START/FINISH:
Bishopstone, Wiltshire SU245836. The X47 and X48 Ridgeway Explorer serves Bishopstone on Sundays and bank holidays from April to October, as does the 47 and 47A bus service between Swindon and Newbury during the week

DISTANCE/ASCENT:
15 miles (24km), 568ft (173m)

APPROXIMATE TIME:
7 hours

HIGHEST POINT:
908ft (277m) on Liddington Castle SU209797

REFRESHMENTS:
Until Liddington, nine miles out, there are no refreshments. In Liddington there is the Village Inn, then in Wanborough besides the Brewers Arm, the Harrow Inn and the Plough Inn there is a village store and post office

ADVICE:
There are no car parks in Bishopstone village so you will have to park on the street, so be considerate. The only source of refreshment being at nine miles, you should carry drinks and possibly snacks or chocolate

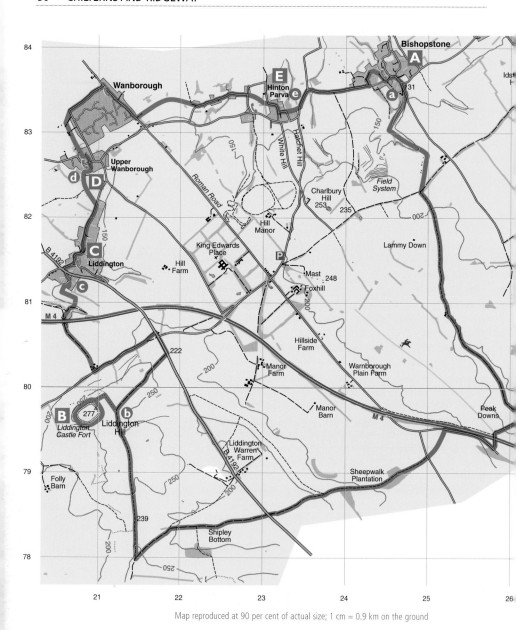

Map reproduced at 90 per cent of actual size; 1 cm = 0.9 km on the ground

right to cross the M4 on a bridge, then right onto the main road, the B4192. Here I saw summer harebells on the motorway embankment to my right. Cross the road to a bridleway sign and work your way right down the road's embankment and through a gate to turn left, head alongside a post and rail fence to the valley floor with a view to Aldbourne on the left.

Across the road, continue along the byway, now a grassy track with crops on the right and a tree belt on the left, beech with ash and some oaks, which thickens out into a wood, the track going through a projection from it, climbing steadily, now along the right-hand edge of the beechwoods. Straight on through gates, descend steeply down Sugar Hill and cross the road to continue on the byway, now the Ridgeway Route for Vehicles. This climbs steadily with occasional sarsen stones alongside and, in the summer verge, toadflax, meadow cranesbill, white campion, yellow vetch and trefoils. The track goes left and hedging appears with agrimony and ladies bedstraw in the summer verges. At the summit turn sharp right onto the Ridgeway Path with Liddington Castle in view ahead. Beside the path is a linear earthwork of the Grim's Ditch type, visible on the climb steadily to the crest. Descend and go left beside the wire fence, through a gate onto the permissive path to Liddington Castle. Through a kissing gate turn left into pasture and walked to the castle, where I noted a painted lady butterfly on a cowpat, and enjoyed the spectacular views to the north and to the west.

Looking back down the dry valley to Bishopstone from the Ridgeway Path

B   Liddington Castle, an Iron Age hillfort has a deep ditch surrounded by two ramparts and these enclose about eight acres, so it is not the biggest but its commanding position where the Marlborough Downs turn east to become the Berkshire Downs gives it greater visual presence. A walk round the ramparts can be most bracing in windy weather.

b   Retrace your steps to the Ridgeway Path and follow it with an isolated clump of beech in the crops to the left with a World War II pillbox in front. Reaching a road, the Ridgeway Path turns left onto it and soon turns right. Ignore this and turn left just past a bus stop. Here there are thorn, maple and blackthorn hedges admixed with rose hips and black bryony with meadow cranesbill in the verges in the summer. Just before a barn at a footpath sign, go right over a stile, the path skirting the ruined farmbuildings, then left over a stile and across pasture to a stile and turn right to descend a dry valley towards the M4 alongside a post and wire fence. Under the M4 head for a black footpath post, descending steps to cross the dry stream and up along a post and wire fence out of the valley, the path turns right to head for Liddington church. You will have to jink right into the recreation ground, left through a gate and along a lane to actually get the last few yards to the churchyard.

Liddington Castle ditch

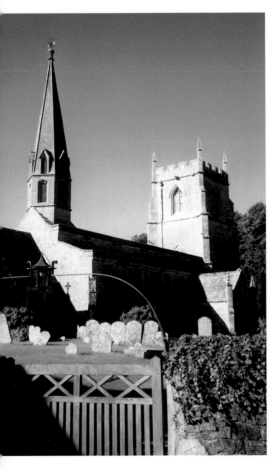

St Andrew's Church,
Wanborough with its two
towers

C   All Saints church, Liddington, is mainly from the 13th Century, with a 15th-Century west tower, but was heavily restored in the 1880s. Inside, there is a Norman font. The Manor House, a Jacobean building with mullioned and transomed windows, is to the east of the village in grounds with a small lake.

c   From the church continue downhill to the main road, walked down The Street, left down Bell Lane past the Village Inn, to follow the road, Ham Hill, which becomes Ham Road leaving the village. In the summer banks are meadow cranesbill and red campion. There is excellent medieval ridge and furrow corrugating the left hand-field and, at a footpath, climb a stile to head diagonally right to a gate amid trees, walking across ridge and furrow. Through the gate continue uphill to a stile, then along a path by allotments to the churchyard of St Andrew, Upper Wanborough.

D   Wanborough Church is extraordinary for it has an octagonal tower with a 14th-Century stone spire above the east end of the nave – itself looking a bit odd – and a large west tower, which was begun in 1435. The legend is that a man promised to donate a spire if his wife had a girl and a tower if she had a boy. She had both, so two towers exist. Wanborough is on the Roman road from Silchester to Gloucester, known in later years as Ermin Way, and there was a Roman settlement here, Durocornovium.

d   Leave the churchyard at the north-east end through gates with an overthrow carrying a lamp. Turn left at a telephone kiosk, past the old school house, right into Mayfield, then left onto a public footpath (the left hand one that descends, not the right hand one). The path becomes a concrete one beside a small stream in a sunken way, overhung by hazel and ash. The path continued straight on and then into Woodland Trust new plantings to head diagonally right to a kissing gate to the left of houses. Carry straight on down Rotten Row to a mini roundabout with the Brewers Arms, a thatched pub on the left

of the junction and The Harrow Inn on the right, also thatched.
Turn right along the main road, a part of Ermin Way, passing the
Plough Inn, and just beyond the village name and de-restriction
signs turned left, the footpath sign a trifle hidden, to climb
between gardens. At the end, climb a stile into pasture to head
diagonally right, over a stile and through nettles. Walk along the
right hand side of a hedge following it uphill, through the hedge
and east across a field, past a sycamore copse, then a farm
access to a lane, turning left into West Hinton. West Hinton
House in chalk stone is dated 1727 with mostly sash windows.
At a T-junction, City Corner, pass straight across to a tarmac
footpath through crops and pony paddocks to emerge through a
kissing gate by the Mission Hall of 1911, with foundation stones
laid by members of the Keable family. Along the lane and round
the bend, climb steps into the churchyard to the right of a very
large holm oak.

E   St Swithun, Hinton Parva, is an excellent little church with a
Norman tower and a fine Norman font. There is a well-polished
late-19th Century bier with large wheels in a corner of the nave.

The porch at Callas Hill Farm, Lower Wanborough

e   Out of the churchyard continue left through the village and
onto a gravel drive to the left of Little Hinton Farm, which
becomes a grassy track past a cemetery, then through two fields
Reaching the main road, turn left to follow it back to
Bishopstone. Past Manor Farm turn left by a very large horse
chestnut to descend West End Lane, then right into Church Lane
with a stream on the right and a chalkstone wall behind. Leave
the churchyard by the opposite corner and at the end of Church
Walk turned left to the mill and millpond.

Coffin Bier in St Swithun's Church, Hinton Parva

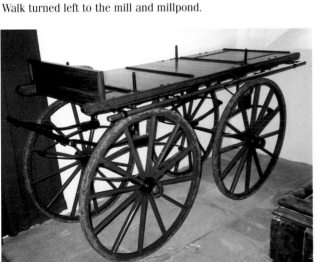

ASHBURY, ASHDOWN PARK AND WAYLANDS SMITHY

MAP:
HARVEY Route Map Ridgeway;
OS Landranger Sheet 174, OS
Explorer 170 Abingdon,
Wantage & Vale of White
Horse

START/FINISH:
Ashbury village SU263850. The
X47 and X48 Ridgeway
Explorer serves Ashbury on
Sundays and bank holidays
from April to October, as does
the 47 and 47A bus service
between Swindon and
Newbury during the week

DISTANCE:
7½ miles (12km)

APPROXIMATE TIME:
3 hours

HIGHEST POINT:
708ft (216m) at Kingstone
Down SU287825

REFRESHMENTS:
In Ashbury there is a village
shop and the Rose and Crown
Hotel

ADVICE:
There are no car parks in
Ashbury village so you will
have to park on the street, so
be considerate. The only source
of refreshment being in
Ashbury you might wish to
take water with you

The walk starts in Ashbury, a good village at the foot of the Berkshire Downs, and heads south across the Ridgeway Path to Ashdown Park, a 17th-Century house set in a hunting park, then back up to the Ridgeway and Wayland's Smithy, an important chambered tomb over 5000 years old. Descending from the scarp the route passes through a deserted medieval village back to Ashbury.

A Ashbury village is built on the spring line, which here is on the lower slopes of the Downs escarpment so the village lanes wind up and downhill in a picturesque fashion amid the chalkstone and brick houses and cottages, the church furthest up the slope and the Manor House at the north end. Its medieval open fields were enclosed in 1772. The latter is a 15th-Century stone house with traceried great hall windows and a porch raised in brick in 1697. College Farmhouse is a good 18th-Century house in chalkstone, with brick dressings and there are thatched cottages, also using chalkstone quarried from the Downs. The church of St Mary is in a steep churchyard with views from the north dominated by its two-storey 15th-Century porch at the end of a cobbled path. Norman, with 13th-Century chancel, aisles, transepts and west tower, the last surmounted by later battlements and simple pinnacles, it is a picturesque composition and inside there is a mural tablet to one Thomas Brown, died 1819. Was this the inspiration for the name of Thomas Hughes' character in *Tom Brown's Schooldays* (Hughes having grown up in Uffington, Walk 7)?

A chalkstone cottage in Ashbury

a From the church in Church Lane, leave the churchyard at its far right hand end to descend to a tarmac footpath, then turn left off it onto a grass path which soon curves right and then goes right uphill with arable fields to left and right. There is little hedge, but in summer the margins have wild flowers including red bartsia, field scabious, trefoil and knapweed, with painted ladies, whites, meadow browns, small heaths, peacocks and small skipper butterflies feeding. Nearer the summit thorn and blackthorn hedges become intermittent then almost disappear with old barbed wire fences to the right to the summit and then to the left. At the top there are views to Liddington Castle to the west and Swindon to the north-west as you walk across the summit of Ashbury Hill to the Ridgeway Path with yellowcress in the verge.

Ashdown Park from Kingstone Down

Cross the Ridgeway Path onto a grassy track with a hedge on the left and a field on the right. The hedge is of thorn, blackthorn, elder and ash with roses, dogwood and black bryony in abundance. The hedge disappears and the woods in the distance on the left are part of the Earl of Craven's hunting park. You will pass a group of beech and horse chestnuts that had surrounded the Red Barn, now demolished, and looking to the left when I walked this path, I could see the brightly coloured parachutes of para-gliders circling Uffington Castle. Over a stile you are in a meadow with one of the three blocks

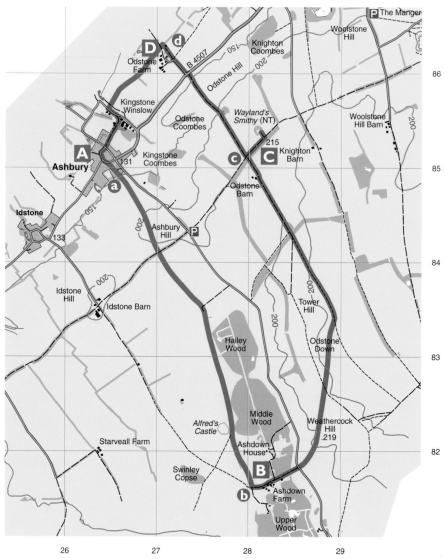

of Ashdown Park's woodland on the left, Hailey Wood, surrounded by the remnants of a stone park wall protected by a barbed wire fence. Within, are some old beech and oak, the rest young regenerating and replanted. Keep alongside a post and wire fence to the right past where the wood waists in before the second block, Middle Wood, also with decayed walling around it, but with more mature beech, ash and oak surviving. On the right is Alfred's Castle, a small hill fort enclosing only about three acres. It is from the Iron Age but appears to have been occupied during the Roman and Anglo-Saxon periods. So maybe there is some justification for its name and certainly hereabouts King Ethelred I and his brother Alfred, later King Alfred the Great, fought a major and bloody battle against the Danish invaders in AD 871.

Continue south past Alfred's Castle, the path becoming a track with the hedge on the left on the line of the park wall with stones visible in the bank or recently exposed by excavation. On the left are now views of Ashdown Park house across cattle pasture and then along a newly planted beech avenue to the west front.

B   There had been a 16th-Century hunting park within a park 'pale', that is a paling fence on a bank to keep the game in when the Earl of Craven bought the estate in 1625. These parks could be used for hunting within the pale but normally the game, usually deer, lived within and were let out through gates to be chased over open country. The hunt could be viewed from the roof of a 'stand', like the Elizabethan timber-framed one at Chingford in Epping Forest, Essex. After 1660, the Earl built Ashdown Park, which was just such a building. From the flat roof of this tall, narrow house the ladies and those who were not hunting could view the chase through the forest around the house and over the Downs beyond. The house is in Restoration or Dutch style with a hipped roof and dormers and a balustraded flat top and belvedere cupola, with

Wayland's Smithy sansen stone screen

service buildings to the east. Ashdown is owned by the National Trust and is open at various times from April to October.

b   At the bottom of the hill the track merges with one from the right and then curves left to pass Ashdown Farm, an old chalkstone farmhouse with stone barns and a granary on staddle stones. There is also a rather grand L-plan Victorian stable building, two-storeyed and multi-gabled and with grooms' cottages and massive, ornate Tudor-style chimney stacks. The woods south of Ashdown Farm are surrounded by a park pale, now an earthen bank and this may be the original 16th-Century park, Ashdown Park itself being the Earl of Craven's enlargement to the north. I had a good view of the south front of Ashdown Park along its lime avenue and then there was a field of sarsen stones along the main road. Along the east side of the road is Kingstone Down, the grassed, steep sides of a dry valley.

Cross the road and go over a stile onto the Downs and take the path indicated by the left-hand finger post to ascend diagonally, eventually passing behind a fenced-off section of young beech trees, at the head of a combe. Head for the ridge beyond a second wired-off enclosure, well to the left of a weathervane on Weathercock Hill. The downs are rich in wildflowers, including harebells, and large numbers of butterflies, blues, marbled whites, tortoiseshells, heaths, peacocks and skippers, as well as a few, five-spot burnet moths. There are also good views back to Ashdown Park. Head to the angle of the fences and out over a stile for a long thrash through almost hedgeless prairies.

Firstly, walk a grassy path through the prairie with redshank, bindweed and knotgrass along it. Straight over a track and across another footpath not visible on the ground, continue descending diagonally to the valley. At a footpath junction turn left alongside a nettley bank and with a steady ascent curving towards a tree belt. A bridleway sign directs you across the prairie with the bank diverging to the right as the parish boundary. Through a beech tree wind break continue straight on to join a track which leads past Odstone Barn, a corrugated iron building full of six-ton straw bales, and through a pine and beech shelter belt to turn right onto the Ridgeway Path to walk to Wayland's Smithy.

C   Wayland's Smithy is actually a Neolithic burial mound or barrow, an earlier one of about 3500 BC incorporated in a much larger one of about 3,300 BC, a chambered tomb with three, stone-lined chambers. In front are four big sarsens set up as pillars and fancifully described as a façade. The site is surrounded by tall beech trees. The name first appears in an Anglo-Saxon charter of AD 955, so is a genuine old one. Wayland was an invisible legendary blacksmith who re-shod the horses of travellers overnight.

c Retrace your steps from Wayland's Smithy to the crossroads where you turn right to leave the Ridgeway Path down a chalky track which begins a steep descent just past a beech copse with good views left into Odstone Coombes, a flat bottomed valley cutting into the escarpment. The track becomes a concrete road and at the main road, the B4507, cross over onto the lane to Odstone Farm.

D Odstone is a deserted medieval village, once a full parish with fields to the north and hill pasture, wood and commons on the Berkshire Downs, a classic long strip parish. Now it is just a farm and with the earthworks of the deserted medieval village around it. The farmhouse is a good one, a late 17th-Century three bay, one with a steep stone tiled hipped roof, the original cross windows surviving at the rear.

Odstone Farmhouse from the north

d Continue straight on past the right-hand side of the farmhouse garden and, passing a cottage, go through a gate and turn left to walk across pasture with a good view of the rear of Odstone Farmhouse. Walk down to a ditch and uphill to climb a stile leading into a field, over stile to walk with a hedge on the left and linnets perching on electricity wires. Cross a track, go over a stile and through a gate left into a short green lane and out through another gate into a lane. This passes the rear of Kingstone Farmhouse built in 1730 and then descends to pass an old watermill, dated 1792, with the duck-filled header pond on the left. Kingstone is another shrunken settlement that once had its own field system and grazing on the Downs. Carry straight on uphill along a bridleway with a view left into Kingstone Coombes and cross the main road into Chapel Lane, back in Ashbury.

UFFINGTON AND THE WHITE HORSE

The highlight of this walk is the chalk White Horse and Uffington Castle hillfort on Whitehorse Hill, but the villages in the Vale below are of high quality: Compton House and Uffington Church are both truly memorable. The walk starts in Uffington, climbs to the White Horse and descends to Compton Beauchamp to follow the spring line east to Woolstone and back to Uffington

MAP:
OS Landranger Sheet 174, OS Explorer 170 Abingdon, Wantage & Vale of White Horse

START/FINISH:
Uffington High Street SU304893 or car park mentioned below. The 47, 47A bus service between Swindon and Newbury serves Uffington week days, as does the 68 between Faringdon and Wantage on Wednesdays and Fridays

DISTANCE:
8 miles (13km)

APPROXIMATE TIME:
3½ hours

HIGHEST POINT:
856ft (261m) at Uffington Castle SU300863

REFRESHMENTS:
There is one pub in Uffington, The Fox and Hounds, as well as a shop. Britchcombe Farm on the B4507 does cream teas on weekends and bank holiday afternoons in the summer. The White Horse pub, Woolstone, offers welcome refreshment at 7 miles

ADVICE:
There is a car park at the Thomas Hughes Memorial Hall at the east end of the village by the recreation field. GR 306896. Alternatively you could start at the car park on Woolstone Hill near Uffington Castle

A Uffington's large mid 13th-Century church, St Mary, is crowned by a tall, octagonal crossing tower and has a complete set of consecration cross roundels on the exterior which date from when it was built and dedicated. The remarkable triangular-headed transept chapels and east porch are most unusual and may date from the 1670s. Inside the church is mostly mid-13th-Century Early English Gothic, with finely moulded crossing and transept chapel arches and capitals, while the Saunders Monument (1603) in the south transept has one of those awkward effigies up on one elbow. South-west of the church is the single room chalkstone school of 1617. This is now the Tom Brown's Museum for Thomas Hughes, the author of *Tom Brown's Schooldays*, was born in Uffington in 1822 and spent his childhood here, his grandfather being vicar.

St Mary's church, Uffington, bathed in evening sunshine

a From the churchyard, cross the road to a footpath sign to walk past the chalkstone-and-thatch Benjy's Cottage on a footpath between gardens and then paddocks. The path becomes a lane, Chapel Lane, past a chequer brick chapel of 1831, to cross High Street into Upper Common Lane, with a reed fringed pond on the left. Just before 'Hookside', turn right onto a nettly path between gardens to a stile. Head south, behind bungalows and climb stile on right. Continue with the hedge on your left over stiles with ridge and furrow in many of the fields. The medieval plough strips fossilised under pasture and survived the common field farming system in use, until enclosure in the 18th Century when the present field boundaries were set. You pass a memorial plaque to the aircrew of a Wellington bomber that crashed in 1942.

Compton Beauchamp House

Next climb over a waymarked stile indicating the path slightly diagonally right across an open field to a double stile ahead. In the next field keep the hedge close on your left again. Notice many next on your right. At the next field junction, ignore the footbridge on the left and go straight ahead over a stile into a young trees plantation of sycamore, ash, rowan and whitebeam amid long grass, then left over a footbridge, then right alongside a hedge with crops to the left. Many butterflies are here in summertime: commas, painted ladies, speckled woods, peacocks, gatekeepers and red admirals. Next comes a thistle-choked pasture with thistledown wafting everywhere and the stream in a valley, thorn, blackthorn, elm and elder scrub along its bank and a wood beyond. Keep the stream on your right and follow it round the bottom of the field to a stile on your right. Climb this, cross the stream, turn left and walk between the hedge and stream on your left and an electric fence on your right, uphill, until passing a gate you reach the main road (B4507).

At the main road turn left to walk past Britchcombe Farm, which does cream teas. Past the farm, turn right at a footpath sign and climb to a stile past nettle-leaved bellflowers. Over the stile, climb in pasture steeply uphill with an ash wood to the right and after two stiles and now on a track, walk through fields to the Ridgeway Path. Turn right onto the Path. Here, a rutted chalky track lies between 18th-Century hedges about 50ft (15.2m) apart: a good width for a drove road. A variety of

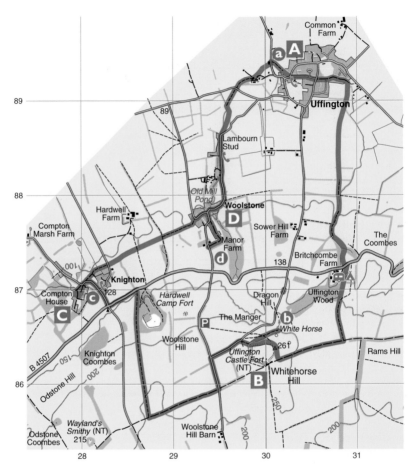

summer wild flowers, including yellow gentian, vetches, field scabious, knapweed, greater plantain with its remarkably delicate, powder blue flower heads and agrimony provided rich feeding for numerous butterflies at this time of year: painted ladies, meadow browns, small skippers, gatekeepers and whites. Continue to the summit, ignoring a stile, and go through a gate to ascend the ramparts of Uffington Castle.

B Uffington Castle is a substantial Iron Age hillfort with a single ditch and ramparts each side and an original entrance on the west. It is at the highest point of this stretch of the Berkshire Downs with splendid views across the Vale from its ramparts. The ramparts were topped with timber palisades, later replaced by a wall of sarsen stones. Recent excavation shows later Roman use. To its east is the most famous feature hereabouts: the White Horse, a gigantic stylised horse, 390ft (119m) long and 130ft (40m) high. It is dated from around 1000 BC and was formed by digging trenches in the hillside which were then filled with rammed chalk. Below is a flat-topped hill, Dragon Hill, which is grassless on top, allegedly because St George killed the Dragon here and its blood sterilised the soil.

b   From the White Horse walk west to the disabled car park and the road, turn left and follow to a T-junction where the road goes right to the Woolstone Hill car park. You go left, signed 'Waylands Smithy' and descend to the Ridgeway Path for about 10 minutes between thorn hedges with meadow cranesbill in the verges. Turning right, walk along the Ridgeway Path for about 10 minutes, passing the parish boundary between Woolstone and Compton Beauchamp, marked by a curving hedgebank running north from the path on your right. At a footpath sign turn right, leaving the Path to cross a ploughed field heading for a gap and a solitary tree straight ahead, then through crops to a stretch between scrubby hedges. If this field path is too muddy, keep along the Ridgeway for another 3 minutes and at a cross-roads, turn left to walk down a tarmacked lane (Knighton Hill) straight ahead across the B4507 to descend to Compton Beauchamp. The path then weaves amid thorn and hazel scrub, draped in ivy, descending steadily with coppice hazel and woods to the right. These hedges represent the double bank boundary between two long strip parishes or manors: Knighton and Hardwell, now absorbed in Compton Beauchamp parish.

Uffington Castle from the west

Over a stile turn left onto the main road and then right at crossroads to descend to Compton Beauchamp between horse paddocks with hornbeam hedges each side and beeches on the left and on the right screening a pink stuccoed house.

C   Compton Beauchamp House has a 16th-Century courtyard plan in a moat with stone and brick elevations. The public view looks along a lime avenue, past gate piers to a cour d'honneur in front of a stone facade of 1710 with giant pilasters. Somehow the whole thing contrives to look French-country-chateau rather than English and is a superb ensemble. Follow the lane to the right past the later 17th-Century service buildings, including an unusual stone tile clad granary, to the church of St Swithun, which has recently been newly limewashed. The church is mostly from the 13th Century, with some high quality 14th-Century stained glass and the chancel walls are painted with foliage by Lydia Lawrence (1900) and modern glass, the rood, screens and font cover are by Martin Travers (1937).

c   Retrace your steps to the house drive, cross the road and go through a gateway waymarked D'Arcy Dalton Way, leaving a wide avenue of new lime trees on your lefthand side. Head for a single-storey, hipped, slate-roofed, Gothic lodge. Leaving the lodge on your right, walk alongside a dense bramble and thistle bank to a stile in the corner beside a gate. Climb the stile and continue with the hedge on your right and crops on your left to a lane. Cross straight over to a stile, somewhat hidden in undergrowth. Ignore the footpath signs which are a little confusing here. The hedge should be on your right side. Continue east to another stile, cross this and the field boundary is now on your left. To your left you can see Hardwell Farm with a moated site.

Continue to a wood and then go left over a stile to skirt the field edge to a stile and footbridge through the hedge some 100 yards (91m) along its east side. Turn left, then in 10 yards (9.1m) go right over a stile to walk with the hedge on the right. The hedge is older than the 18th-Century enclosure. The fields to north and south are bordered by blackthorn, hazel, dogwood, thorn, ash and maple. The hedge carries a tangle of roses, blackberries, bittersweet and black bryony in summer. There is more ridge and furrow in this field and good views south to the White Horse. Go through a gate and another field, cross a stile to the right of a garden hedge into a lane past Upper Farm and you are in Woolstone.

D Woolstone, besides the most welcome White Horse pub, a 17th-Century timber-framed building, is a most attractive village with many timber-framed thatched houses as well as chalk stone ones. It is intimate and has many trees with the mill stream winding from north to south. The former mill house is a tall polychrome brick building of 1877 and the church is at the south end of the village on a no through road. All Saints is a two-cell Norman building with a later bellcote and some good 14th-Century windows.

d From the church walk back to the White Horse pub where you turn right, signed 'Uffington 1 Faringdon 6', to wind north across the stream past good thatched houses along the Woolstone Road. Where the lane turns right there are two options: the first following the road into Uffington is the easy one, the second is to go straight on along a track. I chose to go straight on and somewhat regretted it. Follow this track into a pasture as far as the furthest corner of the field where you cross a new footbridge on your right. Walk diagonally through crops to a stile and a road. Cross the road and straight ahead is a footbridge and what should be a stile. Climb over and turn right to walk along the edge of a hedge, with fields on the left, willows and white poplar in a copse on the right and masses of peacock butterflies on the lesser burdock beside the path in summer. The path veers left of farmbuildings and diagonally right across a cultivated field. Head for a gable of a largish thatched cottage with tall chimneys each side. The path is cut through the crops but utterly choked with redshank, thistles, dock, huge plantains and feverfew. Eventually leave the cottage on your left and cross in front of it to exit to a road. There is a swan sign on the cottage on your left. Reaching the cottage and the road, cross it to a footpath sign and over a stile into pasture to follow the hedge to the churchyard of Uffington church.

The White Horse, Uffington

SPARSHOLT, KINGSTON LISLE AND THE BLOWING STONE

MAP:
HARVEY Route Map Ridgeway; OS Landranger Sheet 174, OS Explorer 170 Abingdon, Wantage & Vale of White Horse

START/FINISH:
Churchway, Sparsholt SU348875. The Sundays-only Ridgeway Explorer bus serves Sparsholt from April to October, X47 and X48, and there is the No 68 Wednesdays and Fridays service between Faringdon and Wantage

DISTANCE:
6 miles (9.5km)

APPROXIMATE TIME:
2½ hours

HIGHEST POINT:
741ft (226m) on the Ridgeway Path at Hillbarn Clump SU325860

REFRESHMENTS:
There are two pubs on this route and no shops: the Blowing Stone Inn in Kingston Lisle and, at the end of the walk, the Star Inn in Sparsholt

ADVICE:
There are no car parks in Sparsholt so you will have to park on the street, so be considerate. I parked in Churchway west of the church which seems the least objectionable location. Again, a straightforward walk with few navigational problems

The walk starts in Sparsholt, a village noted for the 14th-Century oak effigies in its parish church, climbs up to the Ridgeway Path and down Blowing Stone Hill into Kingston Lisle, a village with a country house in an 18th-Century landscape park and a good, small church.

A The Holy Rood, Sparsholt's parish church, has a late 12th-Century nave and a later, shingled broach spire, which looks more Sussex than Berkshire. Inside, the 14th-Century Decorated Gothic chancel makes a visit truly memorable. Here are richly carved stone sedilia (canopied priest seats), piscina, Easter sepulchre and founder's tomb, the last two under cusped arches to their recesses. In the south transept is a rare, early 13th-Century oak screen, and the church also has three oak effigies, rare survivals of Sir Robert Archard who died in 1353 and his two wives. On the way out of the village there are glimpses of Sparsholt Park house to the east behind its stone park wall. This is a seven bay early Georgian house of about 1720 in grey brick with red dressings, segmental arches to its box sash windows and a central pediment.

a From Sparsholt churchyard turn left (south) out of the village with a beech and lime wood on the right. On the left is the stone wall to Sparsholt Park with big beech trees and a box and yew hedge. On the right spindle was in berry, amid maple and elm scrub on the bank, then a modern cemetery within a trim beech hedge. The lane curves gently downhill to the junction with the main road along the foot of the Berkshire Downs, the B4507, passing gates to the southern drive to Sparsholt Park and giving good views of the parkland and the slate roof and parapets of the house itself.

At the main road turn right to walk along it on the verge, firstly on the right and then on the left side of the road. Fifty yards (46m) past a right turn to Westcot, turn left onto a metalled track to climb the scarp of the Berkshire Downs. The track climbs along the edge of a dry valley with initially post and sheepnet fencing on the right, then thorn, blackthorn and elder hedges of varying scruffiness on both sides. Summer wildflowers are sparse nearer the road, becoming more profuse further uphill towards the Downs and include knapweed, bindweed, ragged robin, Indian balsam, lesser burdock, herb robert, field scabious, agrimony, bird's foot trefoil, yellow vetch, red campion and agrimony. At this time of year butterflies are numerous, mostly meadow browns, gatekeepers, whites and some speckled woods, and birds include swooping masses of goldfinches, a pair of meadow pipits, skylarks and yellowhammers. Further on, the hedges are replaced by post and wire fences swathed in brambles, hops, sweetheart and nettles. The track climbs past Field Barn, farmbuildings surrounded by beech trees and scrub and you reach the Ridgeway Path between ivy-choked hedges.

Turning right onto the Ridgeway Path, it ascends steadily as a rutted green lane between unkempt hedges with an excellent range of wild flowers amid the grass in summer, including ladies bedstraw, wild mignonette, melilot, red bartsia, beetroot-red hedge woundwort, horehound, bright yellow toadflax, back medick, wild basil, spearmint and St John's wort. The wealth of flowers of all shapes and sizes attract many butterflies: meadow browns, gatekeepers, small heaths, peacocks and the occasional faded painted lady. This part of the Ridgeway can be extremely muddy in wet weather.

The Ridgeway Path: five ruts and wide verges

The Ridgeway Path gently descends from Hillbarn Clump hill, crosses a road and, climbing gently, leave the Path, turning right at a footpath sign onto a hedgeless chalky track between fields. From here you can look down on the yellow stucco of Kingston Lisle House in its parkland, as well as getting yet another angle on Didcot Power Station's cooling towers. Descend steadily looking at a deep grassy combe on the right with Blowing Stone Hill on its east side. Cross a racehorse gallop, climb a stile to cross the B4507 again.

B Blowing Stone Hill refers to a sarsen stone in the garden of a cottage in Kingston Lisle. This has a number of holes into which you blow to produce a bugle-like sound. The legend is that Alfred the Great used it in 871 when King Ethelred I (not the Unready) and his brother Alfred, not then king, fought a bloody battle against the Danes at nearby Ashdown.

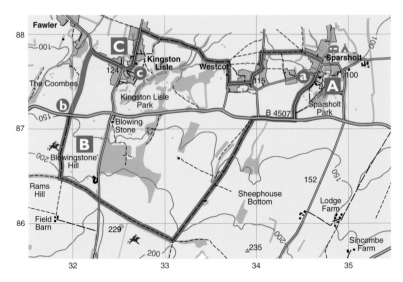

b Across the B4507 go through a gate, then right onto the grassy margin on the right hand side of the hedge. Heading north the path skirts a wood, jinking right and left to a stile. Over the stile, head straight across a pasture corrugated with ridge and furrow formed by medieval ploughing in the village's old, open fields, and now fossilised under the turf. Through a gate, turn right onto a lane with a pavement on the north side alongside an elm scrub hedge with sycamore trees, a contrast to the neat thorn hedge on the right. The lane climbs and then descends into Kingston Lisle.

C Kingston Lisle village is dominated by Kingston Lisle House and its service buildings at the south end of the village

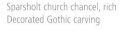

Sparsholt church chancel, rich Decorated Gothic carving

while the main street heads north with several good houses including Thornhill House, a Queen Anne house of brick with cross-casements and a good timber dentil cornice to its eaves. The Church is Norman with graffiti on the north door, and in the chancel there are 14th-Century wall paintings, including a scene showing the beheading of St John the Baptist. The woodwork includes possibly Flemish bench ends carved with initials and the instruments of Christ's Passion, a handsome Jacobean chancel screen and a late 17th-Century pulpit. West of the church, the thatched Little Farmhouse has a 15th-Century cruck truss in its gable. Kingston Lisle House is hidden within its parkland and behind walls. It is a mid-18th-Century house with wings added in 1812 and further altered in the 1830s. Near the church, gate piers with ball finials and a Gothic lodge mark the entrance to the drive and round the corner to the south is the stable yard accessed from the lane, built in chalkstone and crowned by a cupola and weathervane.

Looking towards Kingston Lisle from the Ridgeway Path

c Out of the churchyard turn right to walk through the village past Manor Farm, whose barns are now converted to workshops and the Lonsdale Estate office from where the church key can be obtained. I paused at the Blowing Stone Inn, formerly the Plough, for a drink and continued north, past Orpheus Studio with paintings on display, turning right at a footpath sign onto a metalled track, 'Westcot 1'. This skirts the north boundary of Kingston Lisle Park, much of which is now arable land and screened by a belt of oaks, Corsican pine and beech with a box, fir, hazel, elder and holly undergrowth.

The track crosses a valley with a stream which is dammed within the Park to form lakes. Climb the hill and round a bend on the crest go left of a gate and 90ft (27.5m) to a stile. Cross a sheep field towards the right and over a stile in the hedge before reaching the field gate. Over this stile, turn left along a house drive to turn left onto the lane at the end. Along the lane you pass Westcot Farm with its farmbuildings fronting the lane converted to houses and turn left into Westcot Lane. Walk along the lane to The Orchard, a thatched and whitewashed cottage, and turn right opposite the footpath sign, the path passing to the right of their garage to emerge and cross a field of rape stubble. Reaching the lane, West Street, with former rural district council houses on the left, older ones on the right, you are back in Sparsholt.

At the junction is the Star Inn built in chalkstone with ironstone bands and some brick. Turn right to head back to the church past a course chalkstone wall, to the outbuildings of Rectory Farmhouse. Just before the church, you will find the north drive to Sparsholt House, which has limes and horse chestnuts on the road edge and along the south side of the drive.

The Holy Rood Church, Sparsholt, the west tower and broach spire

THE LETCOMBES AND WANTAGE

The walk starts and finishes in the historic town of Wantage, a borough from 1177, heads along Letcombe Brook to Letcombe Regis and climbs the Berkshire Downs escarpment to Segsbury or Letcombe Castle, a fine Iron Age hillfort. Descending the route passes through the outstandingly pretty Letcombe Bassett and north to follow the old Wilts and Berks Canal back to Wantage.

A Like East Hendred in Walk 10, cloth was important to Wantage. It achieved borough status in 1177 and the market place was in existence by 1284, for then a judge ordered the removal of stalls which had infilled part of the market place. In the late Middle Ages cloth was manufactured in the town and in more recent times the town smelled strongly for it had several tanneries. King Alfred the Great was born there in 849 and his statue, erected in 1877, dominates the Market Square, a long, roughly rectangular space with the encroachment of the sort the judge tried to prevent, at both ends.

a From the long stay car park walk uphill along Mill Street to the Market Place. Right into Newbury Street, past the Blue Boar pub, next turn right into Church Street, passing the very good museum, the Vale and Downland Museum and Visitor Centre, to visit the large, cruciform Church of St Peter and St Paul that dates to the 13th Century, with its battlemented crossing tower. From here follow the road round, Priory Road, passing Tanners Cottages, occupied by workers in the tanneries until 1800. Ignoring the Locks Lane turning, pass the Victorian buildings of King Alfred's School on the left. Arriving at the T-junction, cross to go between gatepiers onto a footpath with a tall yew hedge on the right.

Early 18th Century cross windows in Wantage.

MAP:
HARVEY Route Map Ridgeway; OS Landranger Sheet 174, OS Explorer 170 Abingdon, Wantage & Vale of White Horse

START/FINISH:
Wantage, Mill Street Long Term Car Park SU397880. Wantage is well served by buses from Oxford and Didcot

DISTANCE:
10½ miles (17km)

APPROXIMATE TIME:
4 hours

HIGHEST POINT:
741ft (226m) on the Ridgeway Path at Rats Hill SU378841

REFRESHMENTS:
There are pubs, restaurants and cafés in Wantage, which is a town with a wide range of shops. In two villages on the route there are pubs: the Greyhound Inn in Letcombe Regis and the Hatchet in Childrey where there is also a post office store

ADVICE:
A straightforward walk, the section to Letcombe Regis is on a tarmac footpath. The walk can be completed in one go, with lunch in Wantage at the end. The climb up the Berkshire Downs is short and sharp, but worthwhile. The last section is along a canal towpath, which is easy going

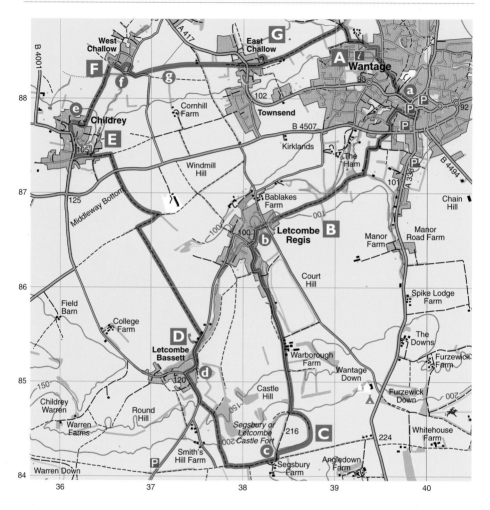

The tarmac footpath crosses a stream and bears right to go round football pitches. Over a stream the path goes right and you walk alongside a cress-filled stream and a tree belt with poplars, ashes, willows and sycamores. After a section through reeds on both sides of the path, reed beds on the right and areas of Indian balsam and meadow cranesbill, the path leaves the stream. Still tarmacked, it heads for Letcombe Regis. It passes through Manor Field, a small estate of former rural district council housing, into the village.

B The Letcombe Brook was a noted watercress producer and many of the cress bed structures survive, but the industry was killed off by over-pernickety health requirements that even concrete-lined cress beds could not meet. Lots of watercress still grows in the stream and the valley from Letcombe Bassett to Letcombe Regis is very beautiful. Letcombe Regis has a winding main street with the church, St Andrew, halfway down and the best lane to the south leading to the Warborough Road with a raised pavement and clusters of good timber-framed and thatched cottages.

b Go straight across the junction with Manor Field to follow the main village road curving to the church near the Victorian thatched gate lodge to Dow Agro Sciences. In the church is a Norman tub font and a lead plaque records a 1737 re-leading of the church roofs.

Out of the church turn right, following the signpost 'Village Downs Only'. The lane winds south and becomes Warborough Road, passing Warborough Farm, a hipped slate roofed farmhouse of the 1850s, built after Letcombe Regis' open fields were enclosed. The lane then climbs steeply up Castle Hill with hawthorn, blackthorn and elder hedges. In summer, the verges are covered with corn mint, betony, cuckoo pint in

St Michael's Church, Letcombe Bassett. An 18th Century tomb and the Norman doorway

berry, vetches, harebells, agrimony, trefoils and ladies bedstraw, among other flowers. At the crest climb a stile on the left onto a permissive walk around the ramparts of Segsbury or Letcombe Castle.

C Letcombe Castle is of course not a medieval castle but a large Iron Age hillfort, with its rampart and deep ditch surrounding about 26 acres. From the ramparts the views are splendid over the Vale of the White Horse northward and include, naturally, Didcot Power Station.

c Leave the castle at the stile, having walked the eastern half of the ramparts, and turn left onto the metalled track then right onto the Ridgeway Path: here a chalky metalled track between unkempt thorn, blackthorn and elder hedges draped in black bryony. Past a beech windbreak on the left, climb a stile on the right to leave the Ridgeway Path. There is another good view over the Vale as you descend across a hay meadow aiming to the left of a wood. Over a stile continue downhill alongside the wood, mostly ash trees but further on also with yew trees and spindle in berry, its edge the parish boundary between the two Letcombes with a distinct bank to mark it. Cross a good dry valley and at the lane turn right to descend into Letcombe Bassett.

D Letcombe Bassett appears in Hardy's *Jude the Obscure* as

Charles Cottage, Childrey

'Cresscombe', a reflection of its main livelihood apart from farming. This is the best village on the walk with some superb cottages, farmhouses and barnyards, picturesquely grouped north of and beside the church in its graveyard. A cruck house at the junction is thatched with its timber-frame infill panels, limewashed yellow ochre. The church is Norman, although the nave and south aisle were rebuilt by Butterfield in 1861.

d Follow the village road round to the right, signposted Letcombe Regis and Wantage, passing more barns, downhill in a sunken way to the Letcombe Brook with old cress beds on the left and pollarded willows on the right. Climb out of the valley and turn left at a footpath sign opposite The Thatched Cottage, onto the bridleway to Childrey. At a path T-junction, turn right onto a green lane which goes downhill between unkempt thorn hedges. At the bottom of the lane, turn sharp left to skirt a long curving bank on a grassy track. Across the B4507 Wantage Road and at a path T-junction, turn left onto a tarmac path to walk into Childrey and at the Hatchet pub turn right.

E In the centre of Childrey's village green with its pond is a Victorian former Working Men's Club and Reading Room and beyond in Church Row is a stone plaque informing us that Sir George Fettyplace augmented the salary of the village schoolmaster in 1732, a salary apparently set in the reign of Henry VIII. St Mary's church has a tall aisleless nave and transepts, with the porch crammed into the angle between.

e From the church, walk back to the junction and carry straight on past a good row of Victorian Gothic cottages attached to the old schoolhouse. The lane becomes a metalled track and where it bends sharp left pass between posts to turn left onto a path tarmacked all the way to West Challow, crossing the reed-filled canal bed by a footbridge and turning right at a lane into the village.

F West Challow is a small village with its lanes circling the Childrey Brook. The church of St Laurence in the centre has an original 14th-Century bellcote.

f Turn left off the lane into the churchyard and then carry on east along the path to a lane where you turn right by some old barns and follow the lane, turning left, signposted Childrey and Lambourn, to a footpath sign on the left to join the canal footpath.

G The canal is the Wilts and Berks Canal which branches from the Kennett and Avon Canal near Trowbridge, heading for the Thames at Abingdon via the Vale of the White Horse. Fifty one miles in length, it was designed by William Whitworth and completed in 1810. The railways caused its decline and now much of it is waterless.

Victorian Gothic cottages in Childrey

g After a section under muddy restoration the canal is more natural with duckweed in some sections, reeds and a thick hedge on the left of the towpath. As might be expected its course is a bit of a nature reserve and speckled woods, peacocks feed on thistles, red admirals on the lesser burdock.

Divert briefly into East Challow to visit the church – medieval with a Victorian west front. Also worth a visit are the grand, former mill and factory of 1840, north of the canal. Made of stone with two, four-bay wings flanking a higher central bay with a carriage arch, now infilled, below a monumental Baroque style cornice and ball finials.

Follow the lane on other side of main road to rejoin the canal. Follow it eastward, leaving it where a tarmac lane crosses to turn right across the canal. Continue along the track round a field edge, until it reaches a housing estate on the outskirts of Wantage, then turn left and skirt the estate until a main road, Denchworth Road, is reached. Follow it south for a short way, then turn left down Belmont onto a footpath to descend into town. The path emerges by a stone pier; cross the lane to Mill Street with the old mill on the right, turn left and shortly left again to the car park.

The Wilts and Berks Canal in East Challow

THE GINGE BROOK, ARDINGTON AND LORD WANTAGE'S LOCKINGE

This walk combines a row of beautiful villages built along the banks of a series of winding streams issuing from springs at the foot of the Berkshire Downs and merging between West and East Hendred to head north to the River Thames. Waterways always makes for an attractive walk and this is combined with some fine sheep pasture on the way up the scarp slope to the Ridgeway Path and good parkland on the way down.

A The walk starts in West Hendred, the junior partner of nearby East Hendred which had prospered mightily in the Middle Ages, having a market charter and being famous in the 15th Century for its cloth fairs. Holy Trinity church, West Hendred, is delightfully situated on the edge of the valley of the Ginge Brook at the southern end of this winding village. Set in a churchyard with lichen-covered tombstones, the medieval parish church has a fine ashlar porch with graffiti cut in by idle hands, one dated 1671. The nicely unrestored interior has a good Jacobean pulpit and there are many fragments of medieval stained glass in the windows.

a From the church go through the modern tile roofed lychgate past the Victorian former school, now a house, to the junction turning right by Glebe Cottage, a timber-framed, jettied and thatched 17th Century cottage, to walk south, soon passing the rear of Glebe House, a hipped slate roofed rendered house with its service wings towards the road. On the left is the mound of Goldbury Hill. Just before a modern cottage, Cedar Cottage, turn right at the footpath sign 'East Ginge 1', climb the stile and descend between a post and wire fence on the right and a garden hedge on the left. Over another stile, pass chicken runs and the path, now a grassy track, passes through allotments, curving right down to the trees that line the deep cut valley of the Ginge Brook. Turn left to follow the edge of the arable to a footpath crossroads flanked by meadow cranesbill in summer and one of this beautiful blue flower's favourite locations. Carry straight on along the path which runs parallel to the stream in cleared woodland with the stream fringed by ash and horse chestnuts. Walk through elm, elder and thorn scrub liberally larded with nettles and hogweed, then through muddy woodland and, reaching a lane, turn left uphill in East Ginge.

MAP:
OS Landranger Sheet 174, OS Explorer 170 Abingdon, Wantage & Vale of White Horse

START/FINISH:
Holy Trinity Church, West Hendred SU447882. West Hendred is served by the 32, 32A, 32B, 36 and X35 bus routes from Wantage, Didcot, Abingdon or Oxford, but as with most rural services you need to check timetables

DISTANCE:
7½ miles (12km)

APPROXIMATE TIME:
3 hours

HIGHEST POINT:
679ft (207m) on the Ridgeway Path at East Ginge Down SU446851

REFRESHMENTS:
The only refreshment is in Ardington towards the end of the walk at the Boar's Head pub in Ardington. Also off the route at the north end of West Hendred village on the main A417 is The Hare

ADVICE:
No navigational problems on this walk, only a short ascent of the Berkshire Downs escarpment, followed by a descent back to the spring line and stream-side villages. Do bring water as the pubs are at 6 miles into the walk

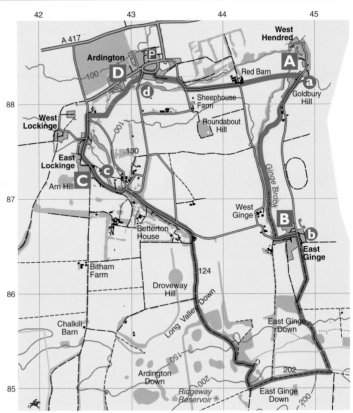

A friendly horse in East Ginge

B The Ginges are little more than a few farmsteads at the head of the Ginge Brook's shallow valley, which forms the parish boundary. West Ginge is therefore within West Hendred parish and East is in East Hendred – its manor house is partly 17th Century, now with a mainly Georgian appearance.

b At the end of the lane past stables, by a telephone box, turn right, signed 'Bridleway The Ridgeway 1' and walk south along a metalled track with crops on the left and friendly horses in paddocks on the right. The track bears right and merges with one coming from the right and head towards a gate into excellent ancient sheep pasture that climbs the escarpment. The track winds uphill to go between clumps of trees over the brow. Below the clumps Grim's Ditch crosses the pasture (see Walk 24).

Beyond the clumps go through a gate, crossing racehorse training gallops, and through a gate to turn right onto the

Ridgeway Path along the crest of the Downs and the highest point of the walk. In the summer afternoon, small skippers and gatekeepers fed on the field scabious alongside the track. Ignore a bridleway sign pointing right to continue past a beech wood with some pines mixed in and, just past it, turn right at a bridleway crossroads to leave the Ridgeway Path.

Follow a metalled track that curves along the edge of the wood and then through it with rosebay willowherb in sunlit clearings amid new plantings. The track leaves the wood and continues descending through parkland with numerous small copses and tree clumps of Corsican pines and beech planted by Lord Wantage in the late 19th Century. The track, still descending, enters beechwoods again which thin to a triple row of beech on the left. Becoming a hedged lane the route swings left to walk alongside a deep valley hidden by trees, the grounds of Betterton House, the stream their centrepiece with cascades and small lakes as well as fine specimen trees. You pass good 19th-Century iron gates between 18th-Century brick piers, the drive to Betterton House, itself occupying part of the site of the deserted medieval village of Betterton.

Sheep on East Ginge Down

Continue downhill with East Lockinge Park ahead behind a low stone wall and then turn left across a bridge over the stream. Follow the road round, on a pavement, to turn right to the church at a sign on a gatepier. The church sits amid the parkland and in good weather the setting is truly picturesque, with sheep grazing in the churchyard and cattle in the park. The stream is a vital part of the park, with rock formations providing extra drama.

C Lord Wantage's Georgian mansion at East Lockinge was demolished in the 1950s, but the orangery remains: a curiously stark 18th-Century brick building of seven tall bays

All Saints Lockinge seen across the lake

sitting somewhat isolated to the east of the church. The church in its sheep-cropped churchyard is splendidly situated and to the north side is a pair of elegant wrought iron gates through which his lordship entered the church. To the south are two medieval style grave slabs, Lord Overstone, died 1883, and his wife Harriet, died 1864. East Lockinge is a model village erected around 1860 by Lord Wantage, some of its estate cottages in a timber-framed style, others brick with unusual dormers and timber gabled porches. The village is now administered by a trust set up by the current landowner, Christopher Lloyd, in the 1970s which has revived the village dramatically with industrial and craft workshops providing work: the whole place is thriving.

c From the church, retrace your steps to the road and follow it alongside the park with its lake and rocky 'cliffs' by the road and through East Lockinge where the old horse drawn early 19th-Century, village fire engine is preserved in a building on the right. At the Lockinge village sign turn right at a footpath sign onto a path. Across the stream on a rustic bridge turn left through a gate and follow a grass path which goes straight while the steam meanders along on the left. Through a gate carry straight on, crossing another rustic bridge, then past a lake on the right and at the lane go left to Ardington church.

D Ardington's church of Holy Trinity looks Victorian with its spire and tower of 1856 and 1887 north chapel, but inside there are some good medieval features. In the churchyard are some pretty odd graves, one to a soldier has his three mourning children kneeling at the feet of his effigy. East of the village centre Ardington House is a good Baroque house of 1721, three storeys, seven bays with a central pediment and built in yellow brick with extensive red brick dressings, parapets and a hipped slate roof.

d Out of the churchyard, continue along the road past the Boar's Head pub and the entrance gates to Ardington House. Turn right under a low bridge along a path skirting the grounds of the House, giving occasional glimpses of its upper storeys over the wall. Reaching a lane turn right opposite No 53, a mid 17th-Century timber-framed house. The lane curved downhill and becomes a metalled track. Cross a stream and turn left onto a farm lane and, beyond Red Barn, modern farmbuildings, the track became a grass one. Trees ahead line the Ginge Brook where you cross on a stone footbridge and up to a kissing gate into the churchyard of Holy Trinity church and the end of the walk.

Bereft children mourn for ever at their father's feet in Holy Trinity churchyard, Ardington

THE ILSLEYS: A STROLL AMID THE GALLOPS

MAP:
OS Landranger Sheet 174, OS Explorer 170 Abingdon, Wantage & Vale of White Horse

START/FINISH:
East Hendred Down Car Park on Ridgeway Path SU458850. There are no buses, but the walk could start at Chilton, East or West Ilsley, both served by buses, Chilton by the 134, which runs from Didcot Parkway railway station, and the Ilsleys by the X48 (the Ridgeway Explorer on Sundays and Bank Holidays from April to October) or during the week, the 234

DISTANCE:
12 miles (19km)

APPROXIMATE TIME:
5 hours

HIGHEST POINT:
660ft (201m) at East Hendred Down Car Park, the start of the walk

REFRESHMENTS:
Several pubs exist en route: the Rose and Crown in Chilton itself and three in East Ilsley

ADVICE:
Take valuables with you if you park on the Ridgeway Path. The Berkshire Downs are expansive with a gentle escarpment, so there are no stiff climbs or descents

This walk includes three good Berkshire villages, one of which, Chilton, was annexed by Oxfordshire in 1974, but the best of the three is undoubtedly East Ilsley, which has a couple of superb early 18th-Century houses. Up on the Berkshire Downs the route crosses or passes numerous gallops for racehorse training and there are long views north from the ridge with Didcot Power Station prominent.

A The walk starts at the small car park at the top of the lane up the escarpment from East Hendred. Six hundred yards east of the start you can look down over the 20th Century's major contribution to views off the Berkshire Downs: Harwell International Business Centre and the Rutherford Appleton Laboratories, sprawling but low-rise, and beyond them Didcot Power Station. Didcot's cooling towers, originally planned as eight and later replanned as six, were separated into two groups of three, apparently to make them less prominent in the landscape, when the coal-fired power station was built and opened in 1970. Harwell started life in 1946 as the Atomic Energy Research Establishment and at one time had gobbled up over 400 acres. Some of that is now being restored by the UK Atomic Energy Authority, clearing redundant buildings, plant and buried waste before landscaping sites.

a From the car park walk east along the Ridgeway Path, enveloped in chalk dust by speeding quadbikes, and, ignoring the right angle bridleway to the left, take the diagonal one left

Didcot Power Station from East Hendred Down

just beyond, signed 'public right of way' and with a new copse of ash, maple and rowan in the right-hand angle. The track descends with red bartsia, wild mignonette, melilot, trefoils, bindweed and agrimony in the summer verges. Past a copse the track descends steeply, then there are horse paddocks on the left. The grass track becomes metalled at the access to Ridgeway Farm and then passes Upper Farm which has a lot of stables. The track becomes tarmac and is a long straight thrash to the road junction with Harwell International Business Centre to the left and a proud sign telling me about the UK Atomic Energy Authority's restoration projects. At the junction with the Horse and Jockey B&B establishment on the left, turn right and then left onto a path that crosses the A34 on a smart footbridge known as Jubilee Bridge and opened in 1977. Across the bridge, go left along the road and then right onto a tarmac footpath past the recreation ground to the Village Hall access and then into the churchyard of All Saints in Chilton.

The village Green pump in Chilton

B   All Saints, Chilton, is partly Norman and early 13th Century, with a Victorian west tower and a gruesome vestry with 1960s casement windows and cement-rendered walls. Fortunately the village has a number of most attractive cottages and there is a restored Victorian parish water pump, painted a cheery green, on the small triangular village green.

b   Walk down Church Hill from the churchyard, past the Green with its water pump and down Main Road to the Rose and Crown pub, carrying straight on past the cul-de-sac sign and into South Row (not The Orchids). Leaving the houses behind, the lane becomes a metalled track then, where a footpath goes left, changes to a green lane between hedges of hawthorn, blackthorn and elder draped in brambles, wild roses and hops. In August, the verges are rich in chalkland wild flowers, including agrimony, bindweed, knapweed, black medick, St John's wort, toadflax, hawkweed, white and red campion, wild mignonette, black bryony and dwarf spurge, with peacock, meadow brown, gatekeeper and white butterflies feeding everywhere.

Continue on the track, ignoring a footpath off to the right, passing a newly planted traditional mixed hedge on both sides of the track, now along a parish boundary. At a metalled track, turn left and head straight on ignoring turnings and cross paths, gradually converging on the track bed of the old Didcot Newbury and Southampton Railway. At a brick railway bridge turn right onto a track and then almost immediately take a right fork onto a grassy track which gently climbs Compton Down

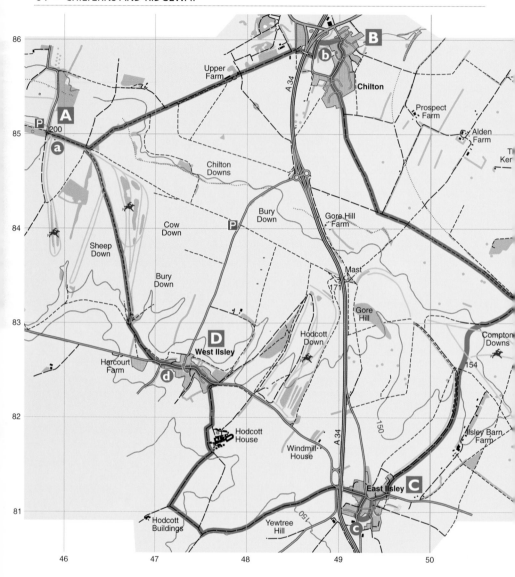

with a Bronze Age barrow just below the brow on the right, Fox Barrow. At a post with a white arrow, also just below the crest, turn left off the track onto a path through arable land and across horse-race gallops, some sand and some grass.

Cross over the Ridgeway Path to begin a steady descent to East Ilsley with occasional bright blue clumps of chicory beside the track. To the right, a wood-chip gallop runs parallel to the track virtually all the way to the village which appears when rounding a bend with the church tower prominent. In August, there was bittersweet on the right, tangled with bindweed and thistles, chicory and, nearer the village, the more intense blue flowers of the meadow cranesbill. The noise of the A34 which mercifully by-passes East Ilsley can be heard a mile away up the track. At the road, turn right and then left at the pond to walk uphill towards the church.

East Ilsley Hall: virtuoso early Georgian brickwork

C East Ilsley was once an important town at the meeting place of numerous sheep-droving routes and received its royal charter in 1620. Sheep fairs were held every fortnight from April to October until 1934 and indeed the market was second only to London's Smithfield, auctioning, up to 80,000 sheep a day. In the centre of what is now a village is a short cross road with two outstanding early 18th-Century houses: East Ilsley Hall on the north side is a virtuoso display of brick: grey brick dressed with soft, red-rubbed brick for arches and dressings including pilasters, window aprons and cornices, all in a Baroque style of about 1720, with box sash windows. Opposite is Kennett House, all red brick of about 1700 with a splendid shell hood on carved brackets over the door. St Mary's church is mostly from the 13th Century with a north aisle and porch of 1845, the older walls rendered.

c Leave the churchyard over brick steps across the west boundary wall into sheep pasture and cross to a kissing gate. Turn right to walk downhill back to the village centre, past the old milestone to reach the Swan and the Crown and Horns, the latter with a plaque dating the building to 1890, a rebuild of a 1759 inn for Hawkins & Co Entire (ales). The road here was widened in front of the Crown and Horns by the demolition of a butcher's shop. At the junction turn left and walk under the A34 bridge.

Immediately through go straight over the road junction onto a track, the Woolvers Road, now a byway which climbs gradually up to Windmill Down, with meadow cranesbill, agrimony, scabious, poppies and hawkweed alongside in summer. The track then descends with hedges on both sides, although scruffy and sometimes meeting overhead. A track merges from the right and after a further 110 yards (100m) turn right at a public bridleway sign to ascend between hazel and thorn hedges. At a junction, go straight on along a footpath that climbs towards a wood with a thorn, blackthorn and dogwood hedge on the left and crops on the right.

By the oak and ash wood, turn right onto a track to cross a dry valley, turning left at a T-junction with a thick thorn, blackthorn, elder and hazel hedge on the right draped in clematis and brambles, some with nearly ripe blackberries. Beyond is a tree belt, mostly of horse chestnuts, all of which screen the West Ilsley race horse stables. The field on the left gives way to horse paddocks and reaching West Ilsley village turn left. There is a post office at the east end of the village which sells chocolate and other foodstuffs.

D West Ilsley is a long village with All Saints church half way along the south side of its main street. The Victorian lych gate is flanked by limes and from here the church looks very Victorian with a separate roofed north aisle. The nave beyond is medieval, but heavily restored, the angle buttresses resting on sarsen stones. Inside, the nave roof is from the 14th Century.

d I paused for a pint in the Harrow at the west end of the village where an inscription on a bench informed me that Nashwan, the 1989 Derby winner, was trained in West Ilsley. Out of the pub, turn right onto a bridleway, the Downland Villages Riding Route, a metalled track between hedges. The track curves right and the hedges disappear. After a while race horse gallops appear and you follow the bridleway all the way to the Ridgeway Path where you turn left to follow it back to the car park.

St Mary's Church, East Ilsley

BLEWBURTON HILL TO LOWBURY HILL

T he springline here comes very close to the scarp of the Berkshire Downs and the villages are on the lower slopes of the escarpment, separated by an outlier hill crowned by an Iron Age hillfort giving excellent views northwards. Almost all of the walk is now in Oxfordshire but until 1974 it was all within Berkshire.

A Blewbury grew up around a number of streams fed by upwards of 30 springs with a main east west road at the south end, London Road. Modern expansion has mostly been eastward to the B4016 and infilling gaps in the centre. The village is a rewarding one and has many good houses along its winding lanes. St Michael's Church, in the heart of the village, is one of great interest, Norman with evidence of a crossing tower. A new chancel and south aisle were added around 1190, the crossing and chancel unusually for a parish church being stone vaulted. To the west of the church a small cottage is an almshouse of 1738, founded by a James Bacon for the oldest man in the village.

a Park in Westbrook Street and walk north along it, passing several excellent old houses and curve right past a tile-coped chalkstone wall. Past the closing post office go straight on at a small green into Church End, crossing the West Brook on a

MAP:
OS Landranger Sheet 174, OS Explorer 170 Abingdon, Wantage & Vale of White Horse

START/FINISH:
Westbrook Street in Blewbury SU528857

Blewbury is served by the 134 and 140 bus routes, both of which run from Didcot Parkway railway station on the Paddington line

DISTANCE:
10½ miles (17km)

APPROXIMATE TIME:
4 hours

HIGHEST POINT:
604ft (184m) east of Lowbury Hill SU542821

REFRESHMENTS:
There are two pubs in Blewbury, the Barley Mow and the Blewbury Inn which is a restaurant pub. The post office and stores closed the day after I did the walk (August 2000) and it is not known whether it will reopen. In Aston Tirrold there is also a pub, the Chequers

ADVICE:
Navigationally, this is a straightforward walk with bracing downland. It would be sensible to take water as the pubs are only in the northern arm of the walk

Cows contemplate Didcot Power Station from Blewburton Hill

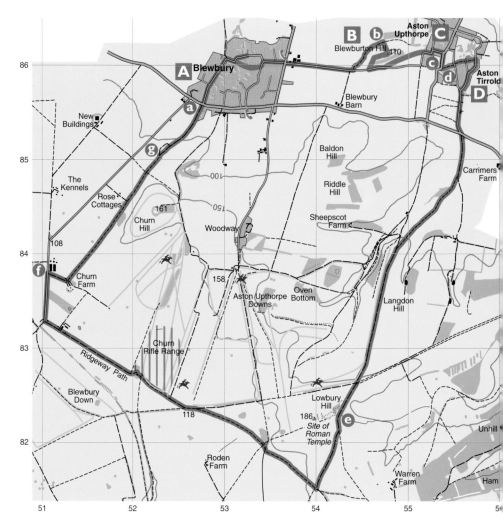

low parapeted bridge, and entering the churchyard part of which is treated as a nature conservation area, judging by the variety of wild flowers within it in summer including nettle-leaved bellflowers and chicory.

Out of the churchyard return to the footpath to the left of the rectory with a stream on the right. Past a thatched cottage and farmyard and a thatched chalkstone wall, turn left at a lane, South Street, and right at the T-junction to walk past modern bungalows on Besselslea Road (not signed). Cross the main road and, passing Winterbrook Farm, follow the track signed 'Aston Upthorpe' with Blewburton Hill ahead, crowned by the splendidly clear earthworks around it. A stile allows you to climb the hill where inquisitive cattle follow your every move.

B Blewburton Hill is an outlier from the Berkshire Downs rising to 360ft and forming a natural defensive site. Excavations showed that there was settlement here, protected by a timber palisade in the 4th Century BC, but soon afterwards it received its earthen rampart and deep ditch. The fort fell into disuse, presumably an era of peace, but was re-fortified in the 1st Century BC, before being stormed and the gateway burned some time in the 1st Century AD, either by the all-conquering Roman armies or in a more local spat.

The guardians of Blewburton Hillfort

b Walk to the top of Blewburton Hill and round its most impressive ramparts, with long views north which inevitably include Didcot Power Station, but also Wittenham Clumps. The fort is also rich in wild flowers in the summer, interesting ones including small harebells, some rock roses and ladies

Good brick and timber-framing in Aston Tirrold

Pigs near Hogtrough Bottom enjoy a bathe

bedstraw. Descend back to the footpath and walk east, skirting the lower slopes of the hill. Leave the wire fenced path left over a stile (easy to miss) to follow a clear path in pasture with a wood along the left on the hill slopes. The small leaded spire of Aston Upthorpe church appears and the path begins to descend to the village, now appearing as a cluster of red-tiled roofs. Out through a kissing gate and down steps, turn left onto a metalled track between Church Farm barns, now well converted to houses.

C Church Farm, Aston Upthorpe, is a rambling old house in colourwashed roughcast with leaded windows and a late 16th Century oriel window on a carved bracket. All Saints church is a small Norman one with rendered walls, a Victorian chancel and lead-clad bell turret with spire. The attractive and gnarled timber-framed porch appears to date from the 15th Century.

c Turn right at the church and the village hall and right again into Spring Lane, which forms the parish boundary between the two Astons. To the left is the Chequers pub.

D Aston Tirrold and Aston Upthorpe virtually merge with the houses on each side of the road in different parishes. On the east or Aston Tirrold side of Spring Lane the United Reformed Church, formerly the Presbyterian Church, was built in 1728. A brick box in more expensive grey brick to the front and sides and red brick dressings it has arched leaded windows and two Victorian porches. St Michael's Church has 11th-Century origins with an apparently reused earlier Anglo-Saxon doorway.

d Immediately past the United Reformed Church turn left onto a footpath which emerges at a road beside a good timber-framed and brick house. Across the road continue on a footpath, across a lane with the path emerging into the churchyard. Behind the churchyard is a high quality house of about 1710, the Manor House, with a shell hood to the door and seven bays of sash windows. Out of the churchyard, turn right to walk south along the winding Aston Street. There is a thatched chalk cob wall on the left and many thatched and timber-framed houses including the remarkably early The Cottage which looks as if it is from the 13th Century and has a restored traceried window to the street elevation.

At a road fork continue south towards the hills along the lane to cross the main road, the A417, onto a public bridleway, leaving the concrete road where it turns left to go right of the hedge into pasture past a gate. During the summer months, it is not easy to spot this path which runs between overgrown hedges draped in brambles and roses, climbing gently, the hedge widening to a hazel coppice with sycamore scrub. Beyond, the right-hand hedge disappears and you walk past pig bungalows with pigs wallowing in their pools with evident pleasure. While I was there a red kite landed on a post nearby and was immediately chased away by two crows. Through an opening in the hedge your track merges with one from the right to continue climbing gently into the hills between thorn and blackthorn hedges which come and go. Wild flowers are in profusion in summer, including masses of harebells and trefoils, rock roses, large and small knapweed, ladies bedstraw and devil's bit. The track descends to cross The Fair Mile and climb the flanks of Lowbury Hill, the highest point on the walk.

e A Roman temple has been excavated on Lowbury Hill and there are several tumuli or burial mounds from an earlier period. Nowadays the slopes are popular with young moto-cross bikers and the whine of two-stroke motors accompanied my climb up to the crest. The path descends to the Ridgeway Path where you turn right to follow it slightly downhill between thorn and blackthorn hedges draped in hops, clematis and black bryony. Side paths by-pass the muddiest stretches: this is quadbike and trail bike country and the hedges are spattered with dried mud.

At a multiple junction, continue on the Ridgeway Path with good chalk grassland margins full of wildflowers. A track merges from the right and again in the summer months there

Blewburton Hill from above Blewbury

is a profusion of wild flowers including ribbed melilot, clustered bellflowers, harebells and rock roses. At the next junction (after about 1½ miles or 2.4km) take the right fork, leaving the Ridgeway path at a public right of way pointer. There are now fewer wildflowers along the track margins but still many varieties. The track passes the ends of gallops and continues arrow straight, sometimes with high hedges. Past modern farm buildings, turn right at Park Cottage with the old railway bridge of Walk 11 to the left. Follow the lane north with a prairie on the left and a belt of young trees on the right: sycamore, horse chestnut, lime and beech, with old beeches at each end.

f At the bridleway sign, turn right onto the drive, past Churn Stables where new brick and flint staff cottages have been built and there of mixed deciduous hedging, gaps in old hedges having been infilled. Past a farm building at the left, turn sharp left to follow a path beside a hedge with a vast field on the left. The path is a steady, gentle climb along the flanks of Churn Hill upon which are two barrows amid the arable. Below on the left, Rose Cottage is isolated amid vast arable farmland. There were beside the path several small skipper butterflies and, under a thorn bush, a clump of petty spurge. The path begins a slow descent with the right hedge bank pocked with rabbit burrows.

g The path reaches a grassy dell with a bench from which to contemplate the fine views northward. The dell is probably an old chalkpit, but the grassy slopes around it are rich in wildflowers including purple Chiltern gentians and yellow kidney vetch in summer. After sitting on the thoughtfully provided bench, continue downhill, the path to the right of the dell, and descended to Blewbury, crossing the main road to complete the circuit in Westbrook Street.

GORING, THE THAMES AND THE EASTERN BERKSHIRE DOWNS

The Ridgeway Path crosses the Thames at Goring, the starting point for this walk, which begins by following the Thames Path national trail before heading into the chalk hills to the Ridgeway Path. From the Path the route heads south into wooded and rolling countryside, more like the Chilterns on the other side of the Thames, through Aldworth, Ashampstead and back north-east to Streatley and Goring.

A Goring was a small riverside village with a Norman church until the railway arrived and, around 1900, experienced another spurt of growth as the river and messing about in boats became very popular, epitomised in Jerome K Jerome's *Three Men in a Boat*. Edwardian riverside houses with boathouses spread along the river banks and the first stretch of this walk looks at many of them from the opposite bank. The church of St Thomas of Canterbury is a complex one. To a Norman nave and tall west tower was added an Augustinian Priory in the late 12th Century, to be completely demolished in the 16th Century.

a From the car park walk past the public toilets to Goring High Street. Cross to the pavement and turn left. Walk across the river bridge from Oxfordshire into Berkshire, passing the Swan Diplomat Hotel which has an old Oxford college barge moored and at Childe Court turn right to follow the waymarks for the Thames Path, another long distance national trail. Walk to St Mary's lych gate to visit the church.

B The main part of Streatley is west of the church around the crossroads at the end of High Street which has some good Georgian houses and a few timber-framed ones. At the A329 crossroads is the Bull, where the 'Three Men in a Boat' had lunch. The church of St Mary has a 15th-Century tower, but the rest is crisp Victorian of 1865.

b From the churchyard, rejoin the Thames Path and follow it along the west bank of the Thames to Moulsford passing Cleeve Lock on your way. This is a most enjoyable two mile stretch of river bank, with Canada geese grazing, great crested grebe, swans with their brown cygnets in summer and along the river bank reeds, comfrey and orange balsam.

MAP:
OS Landranger Sheet 174, 175
OS Explorer No 159 Reading,
and No 170 Abingdon, Wantage
& Vale of White Horse

START/FINISH:
Wheel Orchard Long Stay car-park, Goring SU599807. Goring has a railway station on the Paddington line, reached from Oxford, Didcot or Reading stations. Buses include the 132 from Wallingford, the 137 from Abingdon or Wallingford on Sundays and the Ridgeway Explorer, X47 and X48 on Sundays from April to October

DISTANCE:
15½ miles (25km)

APPROXIMATE TIME:
7 hours including a lunch break

HIGHEST POINT:
610ft (186m) On the Ridgeway Path west of Streatley Warren SU549812

REFRESHMENTS:
Shops are in Goring. The pubs are the Catherine Wheel and the Miller of Mansfield. For the better-heeled, there is the riverside Swan Diplomat Hotel, Streatley, and the smart Beetle and Wedge riverside restaurant and pub, Moulsford

ADVICE:
One of the longest walks, but the pub in Aldworth is about halfway, breaking up the day into a morning and an afternoon section

C Approaching Moulsford, you pass a World War II pillbox built to defend the Goring Gap and behind it a startling modern house by James Outram

c The path turns left through the Beetle and Wedge courtyard to a lane with a big flint wall on the right. At the main road, the A329, leave the Thames Path route and turn left to walk uphill, here in a sunken way, for 200 yards (180m), at the summit thankfully turning right into a byway (sign). The metalled track climbs steadily with marjoram in the banks. The range of wild flowers along this lane is impressive and includes cut leaved cranesbill, goldenrod, dwarf mallow and black horehound. Pass a farm, cross the A417 and go through a gate onto the tarmac lane to Well Barn. The verges, as you gradually ascend the north slope of a long dry valley, contain a profusion of wild flowers in the summer, the most notable being marjoram, harebells, clustered bellflowers, agrimony and bedstraw.

Pass Well Barn, a farm complex, and later a stile. Jink right and left between two shooting lodges, keeping on the main track that climbs through woods, with grouse sprinting and crashing away in all directions. Emerge from the wood on the edge of the valley, labelled 'Cow Common' on the map, but growing crops, with woods along both sides of the valley. Eventually, at a track fork, the route goes straight on as a footpath, through beech and ash wood with box honeysuckle, laurel and hazel undergrowth, emerging at a cottage to follow right, winding downhill to the Ridgeway Path.

Swans on the River Thames

Turn right onto the Ridgeway Path, where there are ancient hedgebanks in the pasture to the left, before leaving it sharp

Streatley Warren looking east

St Mary's Church, Aldworth

by turning left after 200 yards (180m) and following it out to a lane with fine views left down Streatley Warren's dry valley and across into the Chilterns. In the verges are dark mullein and marjoram. Turn left and after another 200 yards (180m), take a right fork signed 'Byway', the metalled track climbing to a lane where you turn left between rich ancient hedges of dogwood, hawthorn, blackthorn, maple, elm and hazel. After 200 yards (180m) turn right onto another byway with small skippers feeding on knapweed and several adonis blue butterflies. The track descends then goes left in front of a plantation of arolla pine, then a range of large weather-boarded barns and ahead is Aldworth church.

D St Mary's church, Aldworth, is mainly from the early 14th Century, but its interior is quite remarkable. It contains no less than eight early 14th-Century stone effigies, six under contemporary elaborately cusped and crocketted canopies. There are two further effigies not under canopies and six are of the de la Beche family. Out of the church I turned left to walk uphill to the present village centre. Here is a shop and the Bell Inn and opposite is a tiled roofed well house, the well sunk in 1868 'by monies raised in this parish'.

d Retrace your steps to the church and carry on downhill left and left again above a grass triangle and then, past Downland Cottage, right onto a byway. Follow this to a road (the B4009) where you turn right, the road and latter part of the track passing through Foxborough Copse, a beech oak and ash wood. Opposite the access to a field the road passes through Grim's Ditch (see Walk 24). The bank and ditch are clear, but obscured from the road by roadside banks. Just before the wood ends turn right down a track which winds through beech woods and a glade dense with thistledown. Across a track the woods become more open with much recently replanted beech. At a track junction, take the left fork and soon descend steps to a sunken lane where you turn left. In a beech, oak and ash wood on the right at a bend, turn right at a public right of way sign.

At a path junction, follow the track round to the left out of the wood and with a belt of beeches on the right. Past a cottage, Millers, turn to the right of a timber garage onto a footpath through a belt of beech, oak, ash and cherry with holly, hazel and bramble understorey. Cross a road onto a bridleway, then after 100 yards (91m) turn left through a kissing gate to cross pasture towards Ashampstead church with its weather-boarded bell turret.

E St Clement's church, Ashampstead, is a small early 13th-Century church, chiefly notable for the 1230s wall paintings inside. At the crossroads, Bloreng House has a former chapel at the back with crowstep gables and a weathervaned turret on its rear wing.

e Leave the church through a gate and turn left to the crossroads. Turn right through the centre of the village, to pass Boreng House and the sports field and turn right down Flowers Piece, 1950s former rural district council houses on your left. At the end through gatepiers, turn left onto a grassy track along to a road. Carry on downhill round a right-hand bend and fork left to a junction by White Cottage where you turn left to follow the road along the valley bottom. After 350 yards (320m), turn right up White Hill, passing a white

The remarkable effigies and canopied niches in Aldworth church

painted brick cottage. Keep straight on, on a metalled track, where the tarmac bears right. Where the track itself goes right follow the footpath sign straight on through pasture and, skirting woods the path enters Bowlers Copse, passing through Grim's Ditch again. Ignoring all path crossings you reach the road (at GR584776) and turn left on to it, then carry straight on where it goes right. Then, when this lane turns left, turn right onto a footpath down the field edge to descend through woods with a notice on the right 'Royal County of Berkshire Shooting Grounds'. Sure enough I could hear guns blazing away in the distance. At a footpath junction at a waterpost in the woods bear left at a signpost to go steeply uphill passing a second waterpost. Soon leave the wood by crossing a stile to walk alongside a fence with grazed out hedge trees along it. At the top of a dry valley and over a stile turn right along a lane which descends steeply. Ignoring a byway to the left, turn left at a footpath sign where the lane turns right into a beech and oak spinney, then into a field to a lane at GR586796, where you turn right. Shortly, at a garden's close-boarded fence, turn left, the path skirting the fence, and over a stile climb steeply uphill in a field to a stile at the top to enter Common Wood, owned by the National Trust.

This wood has beech and oak trees, silver birch scrub, pine trees and numerous grassy clearings. Wild flowers in the summer include the beautiful common centaury. Over a stile follow a hedge, eventually crossing a track into woods via a kissing gate. The path descends to the right of a post and net fence and goes straight on past steps on the left. This stretch is spectacular for the wonderful views down the Thames valley and to Goring church far below. The path descends steeply to leave the woods over a stile. At the road, turn left to walk into Streatley, then right at the traffic lights to walk down the High Street, across the Thames and back into Goring.

St Clement's Church, Aldworth

NORTH STOKE AND IPSDEN

ANorth Stoke village is situated slightly inland from the river on higher ground about 15ft (4.6m) above river level. It is a no-through road and delightfully small and peaceful with the church, unsurprisingly, at the end of Church Lane. The present 13th- and 14th-Century church replaced a Norman one, built for the abbey of Bec in Normandy who owned the church. The tower fell down in 1669 and the upper parts, stone with brick quoins, arches and battlements, date from the 1720s rebuild. Inside are mid 14th-Century wall paintings. In the village there are some good houses, including Rectory Farmhouse, near the church, which has an attractive Georgian facade to a 17th-Century timber-frame and a dovecote in the grounds, the village hall, an Arts and Crafts-style building of 1911, and an old school of 1864.

Approaching St Mary's Church, North Stoke

MAP:
HARVEY Route Map Ridgeway;
OS Landranger Sheet 175, OS
Explorer No 171 Chiltern Hills
West

START/FINISH:
North Stoke SU609862. The 132
and 137(Sundays only) buses
between Wallingford and Goring
stop in North Stoke, the 137
continuing to Abingdon. There is
a railway station in Goring on
the Paddington line

DISTANCE:
8 miles (13km)

APPROXIMATE TIME:
2½ hours

HIGHEST POINT:
377ft (115m) at Hailey
SU641858

REFRESHMENTS:
The King William pub in Hailey
provides the only refreshment
on the route

ADVICE:
A straightforward walk with few
navigational problems. Care is
need in crossing the A4074 and
B4009 at Mongewell. There are
no steep ascents as the Chilterns
are gentle east of the Thames.
There is no obvious place to
park in North Stoke and care
should be taken to park
unobtrusively. This walk can be
very muddy in wet weather

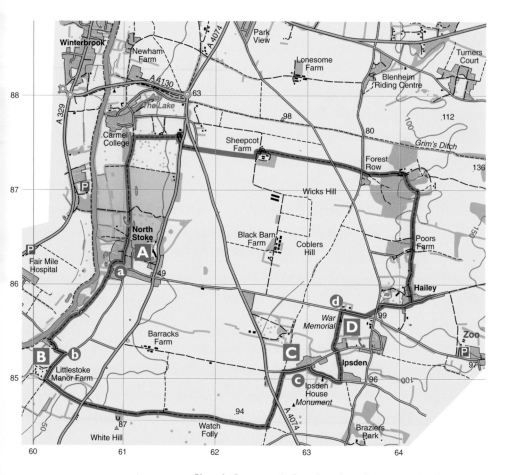

a Church Lane and the churchyard are on the Ridgeway Path, so you follow it out of the far corner of the churchyard through a kissing gate to head south, parallel to the River Thames. The route is through a paddock and, in summer, the dark mullein are in flower and goldfinches are busying about. Then pass beyond a kissing gate past pollarded willows, through another kissing gate where there is arable land on the left and a hedge of blackthorn, maple and hawthorn. In summer, on the right is a withy bed with willows and great willowherb, some teasels and lesser burdock and lots of pretty bindweed in flower. Through another kissing gate, walk between fences and, opposite a long line of horse chestnuts, leave the Ridgeway Path, turning left onto the footpath. Along a gravel drive pass a cottage on the left and Little Stoke House, a white stuccoed house with green shutters.

B North Stoke and South Stoke parishes, the former now within Crowmarsh civil parish, retained their medieval open fields until the 1850s when they were enclosed by Act of Parliament. Until then the villagers had farmed in common with strips allocated in vast open fields in a hedgeless landscape. Virtually all other medieval open field villages had been enclosed by 1800, so the Stokes were late in the process. South Stoke retains the open field atmosphere in some ways as it consists of vast, hedgeless arable fields, bounded only by roads. North Stoke keeps many of the 1856 field boundaries, set out in the Enclosure Commissioners Award, as does Little Stoke itself, which represents the remnant of a separate manor absorbed by South Stoke parish and which had its own common fields running from the Thames to the Icknield Way.

The huge barns at Ipsden Farm

b Reaching the road, turn right, and you will soon pass the good flint and brick walls to the grounds of Little Stoke Manor on the right. The lane bears left and here you get a view of Isambard Kingdom Brunel's wonderful 1839 Moulsford Railway Bridge across the Thames with its unfeasibly shallow arches. On the left is a thorn, blackthorn and elm hedge, which predates the 1853 enclosure. At the B4009 Wallingford Road cross onto a track which also predates the enclosure award, giving access to the old common fields, now part of the Swan's Way long-distance bridle path and signposted 'Ipsden 2½ miles'. Look back to see Didcot Power Station's cooling towers, your constant companion for much of the Ridgeway Path as far west as Liddington Castle.

The track passes through arable land and when the weather is good, there is a good variety of wild flowers in the verges, including black medick, St John's wort, wild hops, wild basil, agrimony, mallow, knapweed, scabious, vetch, mouse eared hawkweed and ragwort. Butterflies include meadow browns, gatekeepers and marbled whites. The track climbs steadily, passing a corrugated iron barn complex at Middle Barn, which looks like the abandoned American mine in a Western, and near the summit a new small deciduous wood, Cameron's Copse, planted in memory of a Jock Cameron in 1995.

The track descends towards the main road. Before the road, turn left at a footpath crossroads to walk through crops on the course of the Icknield Way to cross the main Port Way, A4074, an ancient route followed by parish boundaries for much of its length. Carry on through a field to a horse chestnut copse within which is an early 19th-Century monument within

The porch at St Mary's Church, Ipsden

railings. It is a small stone pyramid above a square base in memory of John Reade, who died in India in 1827, and a brother of Edward Reade of Maharajah's well in Stoke Row fame. Across a footbridge, turn right onto the lane to Ipsden with mallow, wild geranium and white campion abundant in the summer verges.

C   Ipsden, with the small village's centre about a quarter of a mile from its church, is dominated by Ipsden Farm, which has a vast range of brick barns with several waggon porches. Built in the late 18th Century, the size of these barns reflect the enormous production of crops in this area: there is an even bigger one at Fyfield Manor near Benson. This area was (and still is) enormously productive and enjoyed a golden age between the French or Napoleonic Wars and the repeal of protectionist Corn laws in 1846. These vast barns are a physical remainder of that rich era.

c   Past the barns, turn right to pass Ipsden House, a Georgian refronting of 1764 with a Venetian window. Left at a green footpath post by Ipsden Cricket Club, passing in front of the pavilion, walk down an elm scrub avenue to emerge in a field and a nettley, brambly path to the left of the hedge. Across a road, walk alongside a heavily buttressed flint wall, up a steepish lane with sun spurge in the verge to the War Memorial, a Celtic cross and then to Ipsden church.

D   St Mary's Church, Ipsden, is north of the village and, like North Stoke, was owned by the Norman abbey of Bec. It is an unexpectedly fine small church, presumably paid for by the monks of Bec, in an up-to-the-minute late 12th-Century style. Various windows were altered in the Gothic period and the porch of 1634 adds mellow brick to the picture. At the gates is a cast-iron village well head pump, now within a railed enclosure, its machinery by Wilder of Wallingford dated 1865.

d   Out of the church, turn left or east past a pair of cottages with red admirals and small tortoiseshell butterflies in the garden in summer. You cut off two corners of fields by going over four stiles to the lane into Hailey. Continuing past Stone Farm, which has a date of 1677 on its gable walk to the popular King William pub for lunch and a drink.

Leaving the King William, retrace your steps to Stone Farm and turn right up a tarmac lane which becomes a metalled track. Pass Poors Farm, straight ahead with a good two-porch barn (more 18th-Century corn wealth) and at a path junction, note much chicory in bright blue flower. Through a field, enter a beechwood with ash scrub, evidence of bluebells in spring, and a lot of clustered bellflowers while red admirals, meadow browns as I passed in summer. Out of the wood, turn left at Woodhouse Farm, a rendered 18th-Century farmhouse with a backdrop of an oak and beech wood, and a barnyard to the left.

After cottages, Forest Row, leave the tarmac and carry straight onto a track with ladies bedstraw, St John's wort, agrimony and white campion in the verges. Across another road the path goes through a field with knotweed, mugwort, bindweed, groundsel and feverfew underfoot during the summer months. Beyond Sheepcot Farm the path becomes a track with pig huts on the left. Cross the main road to a footpath sign just before a leylandii hedge and descend with crops on the left and a hedge on the right overgrown with thistles and nettles, but also with a lot of spearmint growing. Cross another road with care, (the B4009) to a footpath sign and through a gate descend to a stile into Mongewell Park which has parkland sycamores, limes and horse chestnuts amid the cattle grazed grassland. Continue past former estate labourers cottages to the Ridgeway Path junction where you turn left. The park was the grounds of a Georgian mansion and was laid out in the 18th Century, but is now part of Carmel College, which is discussed in Walk 15.

Follow the Ridgeway Path south, with the Springs golf course on the left beyond tall lime trees initially and on the right poplars, reeds and great willowherb, the river about 400 yards (366m) beyond. After passing through the golf course the path enters an avenue of oak, beech and sycamore into North Stoke. Past the 1911 village hall turn back into Church Lane.

Inside St Mary's Church, Ipsden

WALLINGFORD: AN ANGLO-SAXON BURH WITH A CASTLE

MAP:
HARVEY Route Map
Ridgeway; OS Landranger
Sheet 175, OS Explorer No
171 Chiltern Hills West

START/FINISH:
Riverside Outdoor Swimming
Pool Car-park, Crowmarsh
side of Wallingford Bridge
SU611894. Wallingford is
served by many bus routes
while buses from railway
stations at Didcot, Goring,
Reading and Oxford can
combine with the trains for
walkers to get to Wallingford
from further afield

DISTANCE:
5 miles (8km)

APPROXIMATE TIME:
2½ hours

HIGHEST POINT:
213ft (65m) on summit of
Wallingford Castle motte
SU609898

REFRESHMENTS:
There is considerable choice
in Wallingford, of course, and
near the end of the walk
there is the Queen's Head in
Crowmarsh, the 14th-
Century aisled hall

ADVICE:
This is the shortest walk in
the book and part of it is in
a town, so there are few
navigational or other
difficulties

This walk focuses on the ancient Anglo-Saxon town of Wallingford, whose Anglo-Saxon earth ramparts survive to a great extent, as do the impressive earthworks of the medieval castle, both built here to defend a strategic crossing of the River Thames. Leaving the town, the route follows the river south, crossing it to join the Ridgeway Path to visit Mongewell Church and head north to Nuneham and Crowmarsh.

A Although there is evidence of prehistoric and Roman occupation in the area, Wallingford only became a major settlement in the late 9th Century as one of the 'burh' or fortified towns built by Alfred the Great to defend Wessex from the Danes. Wallingford is included in the 'Burghal Hidage', a document drawn up around AD 919, which provided for the defence of the Wessex military towns. It was one of the largest and it is fortunate that so much of these ramparts survive.

By 1086 and the time of Domesday Book there were 491 houses within the walls, although some had been demolished to make way for the castle and the town had its own mint and market. In 1155 the town received its first charter, and later in the Middle Ages it had 170 burgesses or leading citizens, 13 parish churches as well as a small Benedictine priory in what is now Bull Croft Park. However, its prosperity declined after 1416 when Abingdon's bridge over the River Thames drew trade away and by the 16th Century there were only four churches left. Later, the 17th Century saw a revival in the town's fortunes – the town hall being built in 1670 – and there are some excellent Georgian and early 19th-Century houses within the town, some of them re-fronting earlier timber-framed ones.

a From the open air swimming pool car park turn right to cross Wallingford Bridge, a long, stone bridge of 17 arches, five of which span the river. Three arches are medieval, the three central ones with the balustrades were rebuilt in 1809, the rest to each side date from 1751. Walk up the street from the river passing some fine houses including Calleva House on the left, now an antique shop, an early Georgian house of high quality retaining the original thick glazing bars to the small pane sashes, a tall, pedimented doorcase and pilasters between the windows, the George Hotel, timber-framed and

The George Hotel, Wallingford

jettied, and, at the corner of Castle street the Lamb Arcade, a former coaching inn of the 1730s.

Turn right into Castle Street, walk past the car park and the former churchyard to All Hallows and enter the castle grounds through a gate. From formal gardens with some big specimen wellingtonia, planes, deodar cedars and sycamores, climb onto the rampart of the inner bailey with remnants of corner towers and some 16th-Century walling of the former collegiate church of St Nicholas. Cross the 'drawbridge', a modern one with chains, to follow the zigzag path up the motte to gain views over the castle, the town, the river and the surrounding countryside, in fact the highest point on the walk.

B Wallingford Castle was a royal one and its construction some time in the later 11th Century, involved demolishing houses in the north-east quarter of the town and in the 13th Century it was one of Henry III's royal residences. After about 1385 it fell into decay and remains a picturesque complex of earthworks, some of which were landscaped into gardens, while the bulk of the outer bailey, the northern part became pasture. Some fragments of stone walling remain and the motte, the keep mound, survives. The public grounds were opened to the public in 1978, the gift of Sir John Hedges, a noted local amateur historian.

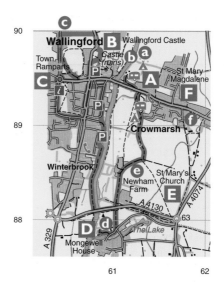

b After climbing the motte, descend and leave the park via the gate and turn right along Castle Street, now with Victorian and Edwardian villas rather than Georgian houses alongside. Just past No 23 where the road curves right, go left down four steps onto a path between chain link fences. On the left is the Anglo-Saxon town rampart and ditch, the focus of the next section of the walk.

C The Anglo-Saxon burgh's ramparts remain almost intact along the west side, the north side as far east as Castle Street (the castle destroyed it from here to the river) and along the south side, almost as far east as St John's Green. The ditch has fared less well and the best stretch, known as the Black Ditch, is in the north-west quadrant. The ditch is deep and it appears that there were never walls along the crest of the ramparts.

c Walk along the north side of the ramparts and, before the houses, turn left to cross the ramparts and ditch on newish steps into Bull Croft Park. Walk along the inner face of the western ramparts as far as you can to where there is a fluted 1830s column relocated here from the Market Place in 1921, when the present war memorial was erected. Descend east to leave the park and turn right into High Street. On the right is Wallingford Museum, a 17th-Century flint building, originally E-plan, but with the centre infilled, the side-wing gables being clear to see. Cross the road and follow the diagonal path right across the park, King Croft, back up some steps to the ramparts. Once at the top, turn left onto the south arm of the rampart. The ramparts gradually diminish and you end up in a lane. Turn left at the Coachmakers Arms and walk up St Mary's Street to the medieval market place, the islands of buildings between here and the Town Hall being an encroachment into what had been a very large and long market place.

The Market Place, now paved, has on its south side the stuccoed Town Hall of 1670 and behind it St Mary's parish church, Victorian except for the west tower. The old cast-iron drinking fountain, presented by Alderman Hawkins in 1885, was taken away as a hazard to traffic, but reinstated in 1979, beautifully refurbished. The houses north of this as far as High Street are also encroachments on the medieval market place and the route leaves via the right-hand lane, turning right into the High Street and second right into Thames Street, now joining the Thames Path long-distance footpath.

On the left is St Peter's Church, a Georgian rebuild of the 1760s, distinguished by Sir Robert Taylor's extraordinary spire above his open octagonal belfry, the spire ogee curving, slender and distinctly non-medieval in style. At the end of the lane is St Leonard's Church, a Norman church brutalised and 'improved' in Neo-Norman style in the 1840s, its churchyard now a nature trail. Go left of the church, still on the Thames Path, over a stream to follow the Thames Path through a boatyard and along the river bank as far south as the road bridge, go right through a gate to a path up to the road, the A4130, and cross the bridge, opened in 1993. On the east side, descend to the right of a track under the bridge to join the Ridgeway Path. Follow the Path as far as a sign just before a row of white-painted flat roofed houses 'To St John's Church Only'. There are way markers which lead through the grounds of Carmel College, a Jewish college, conference and residential centre which moved here in 1953.

The 1885 fountain in Wallingford Market Place

D The present Mongewell House is an 1890s replacement for a Georgian one, but some of the 18th-Century landscape remains amid numerous modern buildings for the college, some of distinction like the 1963 synagogue. Within all this is the old parish church of St John the Baptist, a Norman building in part given the garden-temple treatment in 1791 by Shute Barrington, with a brick nave, slender turret tower and apses. The nave is now even more romantic being roofless, but the heavily restored Norman chancel remains.

Newnham Murren church and farmhouse

d Retrace your steps back to the Ridgeway Path and leave it on a byway, straight under the main road. Carry on along the path between maple and thorn trees with occasional hazels, elder, elm and crab apples and chicory in the verges to Newnham Murren Church.

E St Mary's church, Newnham Murren is isolated in the fields with only Newnham Murren Farm next to it, an attractive stuccoed house with 17th-Century origins, or even earlier. The church is mainly Norman, in flint, heavily restored and with a Victorian bellcote.

e The path meets the farm road and follows the concrete road bearing right. Where the road curves right, turn left onto a grassy track between post and wire fences, a field on the right and pasture on the left. After an occasional dead elm or thorn, thicker hedging appears, mostly elm scrub, maple, thorn and blackthorn, even a single stray walnut tree. Straight on at a footpath junction, now with a campsite on the right behind a row of planes, poplars and alders. There are good views of Wallingford at various points along this path which becomes a track before it reaches the main road. Turn right to Crowmarsh Gifford.

F St Mary Magdalene, Crowmarsh Gifford, on the north side of the road, is another Norman church and again subject to somewhat heavy Victorian restoration. Continue past some good village houses to the Queen's Head pub. The east elevation has its timber framing exposed – the building was in fact an aisled hall house, dendro-chronologically dated to about 1341 and well worth a visit for a drink or lunch.

f From the Queen's Head retrace your steps towards Wallingford Bridge and the car park.

NUFFIELD AND GRIM'S DITCH

On a sunny late December day with the countryside covered in snow, the Chilterns look their best. Even Didcot Power Station, seen at various points on the route, appears mysterious and rather beautiful rising above the snow and lowland mists, its chimneys disembodied, their steam merging into the haze. Walking in snow-covered landscapes on a bright winter's day is at least the equal of a warm summer's day. Instead of wild flowers and butterflies there are berries and birds aplenty. In this part of the Chilterns you would expect to see numerous robins, their red breasts strikingly contrasting with the white of the snow-cloaked landscape, the occasional green woodpecker, wrens and of course soaring red kites, kestrels and sparrowhawks. More gregarious birds seen on that December day include redwing, goldfinches, long-tailed tits, wood pigeon and lapwing: all seen during the walk. Grey squirrels abound, one dashing 20 yards (18m) ahead of me, stopping and looking back before leaping on, this for over a mile alongside Grim's Ditch.

A Holy Trinity church, Nuffield, has Norman origins and an early 14th-Century north aisle with its own separate pitched roof rather than the usual lean-to type. The tower has a shingled bell stage and inside the Norman font has an interesting Latin inscription. This, at the start of the route, is the highest point on the walk.

a From the churchyard, walk west down the lane for 164ft (50m), then left down a path signposted along the edge of a large arable field with a view of Didcot Power Station rising eerily from the snow mist far to the west.

MAP:
OS Landranger Sheet 175, OS Explorer No 171 Chiltern Hills West

START/FINISH:
Nuffield, Oxfordshire SU667873. Nuffield is served by the X39 Oxford, Wallingford, Henley bus which stops near the Crown pub on the A4130 at Nuffield Common

DISTANCE:
7 miles (11km)

APPROXIMATE TIME:
3 hours

HIGHEST POINT:
692ft (211m) Nuffield church SU667873

REFRESHMENTS:
The only pub on this route is the Crown at Nuffield by the A4130 on Nuffield Common. A drinking water tap in Nuffield churchyard offers cool water to refill bottles

ADVICE:
Parking in Nuffield is possible. There are few navigational problems but Grim's Ditch is rewarding

Nuffield Church

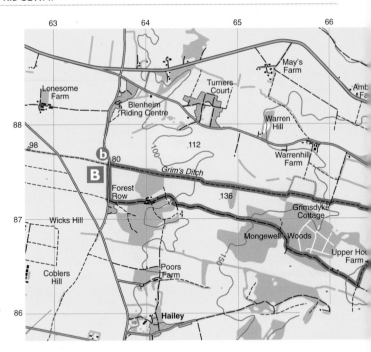

A step stile north of Upper House Farm

Pheasants scatter ahead, dark shapes against the snow. The path descends amid trees and, where the Ridgeway Path turns right onto Grim's Ditch, carry straight on, the path winding amid the narrow tree belt, mostly beech, oak and tall gean. Over two stiles, crossing a tarmac drive before the second, the path skirts the post and rail fence east and south of Upper House Farm, a timber-framed house with a flint and tile roofed outbuilding, a mighty oak next to its pond where the path turns west. In the snow, hare and rabbit tracks can be seen. Turn left at a footpath sign to continue south to a track where you turn right, passing the slate name plaque to Upper House Farm.

Follow this track past what were Upper Cottages, now a modern timber-framed manorial style house. The path then descends through Mongewell Woods, full of pheasant, game birds and pigeon. These woods are ancient oak and hazel coppice woods, now with many conifers planted in the centre, and were at the eastern end of the former parish of Mongewell which ran from the Thames at Mongewell Park (see Walk 15) up into the Chilterns.

You pass derelict sheds and eventually wind out of the woods through a good stretch of hazel coppice and crossing the more recent parish boundary between the north part of Ipsden and Nuffield parishes. The route is now a green lane whose hedges soon disappear with post and wire fencing appearing. The lane winds right past Wicks Wood to descend to Woodhouse Farm in the valley bottom with Oaken Copse behind it, a picturesque group of an 18th-Century rendered and tile-roofed farmhouse and ranges of weatherboarded farm buildings. The lane continues past to meet a tarmacked lane by Forest Row, two pairs of 1920s farm cottages. Turn right onto the lane, here the parish boundary between Ipsden and Crowmarsh parishes, to descend and turn right to rejoin the Ridgeway Path, here following one of the best stretches of Grim's Ditch.

The Ridgeway and Grim's Ditch cross the Icknield Way

B The lane followed the course of the Icknield Way, a very ancient trackway that skirts the foot of the Chilterns and part of a long distance route connecting Salisbury Plain and East Anglia in Neolithic times. Several of the routes in the book, such as Walks 17 and 18, meet up with this trackway. Our stretch of the Icknield Way here passes through the much later Grim's Ditch. We shall walk other stretches of the linear earthworks known as Grim's Ditches or Dykes in later walks further east, such as Walk 24, but this stretch is very different from them.

With a central ditch and a bank each side Grim's Ditch, this fine Iron Age earthwork runs slightly south of east from the Thames near Mongewell for nearly four miles, then disappears before re-emerging for a further mile, a good stretch being on Nuffield Common along the southern edge of the golf course. Although its origins are lost in the mists of time it seems that it formed a boundary between lands of different Iron Age tribal groups or estates, which consequently controlled trade and travel along

Descending towards Woodhouse Farm

the Icknield Way. West of the Icknield Way lane the Ditch is a bridleway, followed by the Ridgeway Path from near Mongewell: to the east, on our route it is a footpath mostly along the right hand bank, but occasionally on the left or in the bottom of the ditch.

The most impressive section, its ditch often fifteen feet deep and the banks each side high above the adjacent countryside, starts beyond Bachelors Hill where the Ditch climbs into the hills. West of the Icknield Way the Ditch crosses more open country, the 'champion' of vast arable fields, the successors to the medieval open fields only enclosed in the mid 19th Century. Our stretch of Grim's Ditch is two miles of excellent earthworks, much of it within woodland or tree belts.

b   The route follows the Ridgeway Path for two miles, passing through three kissing gates, one donated by Abingdon Rotary Club 'who walked the Ridgeway Path 1986–1996' as a brass plaque informs us. By Woodlands Cottage, a painted brick and tile roofed cottage there is a drinking water tap for the use of walkers: not needed amid the December snow, but most welcome on a hot summer's day.

At the end of this stretch of Grim's Ditch the Ridgeway Path turns left and we retrace our steps along it to Nuffield Church, pause for a drink of water from the tap by the church, then continue on the Ridgeway Path which goes left off the lane opposite the churchyard's War Memorial by the iron fence into a field. Across this the path goes via a kissing gate across a golf course, guided by posts numbered one to seven, emerging in the drive to Fairway Cottage. At the road the Ridgeway Path goes left, but you turn right to walk past the Crown, a Brakspears pub.

C   The Crown is by the side of the main Henley to Wallingford Road, just before it descends westward down Gangsdown Hill, this a difficult stretch of the road from Henley to Oxford via

Benson which was turnpiked in 1736. This present route subsequently replaced the 1736 one which survives as a bridleway north of the road, rejoining it beyond Harcourt Hill. It is difficult to realise nowadays as one sweeps up the hill in a car how hard horses had to work hauling coaches up these steep hills in what was then a much wilder countryside than now or descending slowed down by a 'skid' or a long pole pressed onto the road behind the coach.

The Crown has a coursed flint front of about 1800 with brick quoins and window surrounds and a range of attractive outbuildings, its front facing south-east to the common, not towards the main road. Beyond is the bus stop for the X39, while the old common is now entirely a golf course, the Huntercombe Golf Club.

c Near the bus stop is a footpath sign. Follow its direction SSE for 820ft (250m) diagonally across the golf course to a gap in

the tree belt and then across another fairway to the road. Cross this (there is another footpath sign) and head SSW for 984km (300m) across more golf course fairways and tree belts, to a gap between a hedge and a tree belt, the latter with a fine stretch of Grim's Ditch within it. The path crosses the an arable field on

Upper House Farm from the South

the course of Grim's Ditch, here invisible. This stretch was tricky in the undisturbed snow with no way marks visible on the golf course and the snow undisturbed by any human feet, only squirrels, rabbits and pheasant tracks. Snow or not snow, this path is not clear on the ground.

Across the field you reach a tree lined sunken green lane and turn right into it. It is flanked by ash, thorn, oak, hazel and holly, mostly unkempt and ivy choked. Soon you pass between gardens and bear left onto a path beyond Elderberry Cottage, in fact a modern bungalow, ignoring the track which bears right. Follow the path to the road, emerging beside Martyn's Close, a 1950s house in Neo-Georgian style with a plastic shiplap boarded upper floor. Across the road carry straight on, signposted 'Nuffield Church', passing the entrance to the Huntercombe Golf Club and the former Board School of 1870 now (December 2000) being converted into houses back to the church.

Beech leaves amid the snow on Grim's Ditch

BRITWELL SALOME AND SWYNCOMBE

This route takes in some of the best rolling Chiltern Hills scenery at their western end ranging from the vast fields on the western slopes to intimate sheep cropped valleys around Swyncombe. Scenically, the eastern arm of the walk takes some beating while Swyncombe manor and church comprise an unforgettable group at the head of a remote valley.

A The first part of the route out of Britwell Salome, a village on the same spring line as Watlington, Shirburn and Ewelme, skirts the grounds of Britwell House. It must be admitted that winter is the best time to walk this stretch as the house is hidden, except for occasional fleeting glimpses, by dense hedging and trees which include much scrub elm. When the leaves are off you will see the Palladian villa that was built in 1728 for Sir Edward Simeon. It has a pedimented central block flanked by lower pavilions, all with slated hipped roofs and in brick with stone dressings. At the left is a cupolad stable block and in front of the house Simeon set up a tall memorial column to his parents in 1764.

a Start the walk near the Goose pub in Britwell Salome. Between the pub and its car park is a track; follow it past the footpath sign between thorn, elm and hazel hedges. It becomes a path, winding between brick and flint walls, and emerges on a lane beside Chiltern Cottage, which has a side elevation with alternating chalk and flint bands. Left along the lane, turn right at the junction to walk out of the village and, where the lane bears left, go right onto a metalled track with elm hedges and follow the track past the grounds of Britwell House. At a footpath junction turn left onto a track to climb gently south-east; there is a thorn, blackthorn and elder hedge on the left with knapweed, spearmint, agrimony and marjoram in the verges in summer. Meeting a track turn right onto a rutted stretch of the Icknield Way and the Swan's Way long-distance bridleway. The track soon enters a most attractive beechwood, keeping close to the edge of the wood. Within are fir trees and cleared areas with ash scrub and young beech and silver birch.

Out of the wood, carry straight on along a lane with more marjoram and also St John's wort in the verges, then left at a

MAP:
HARVEY Route Map Ridgeway; OS Landranger Sheet 175, OS Explorer No 171 Chiltern Hills West

START/FINISH:
Britwell Salome SU671932. Britwell Salome is served by the 132, albeit not very frequently

DISTANCE:
10 miles (16km)

APPROXIMATE TIME:
4 hours

HIGHEST POINT:
741ft (226m) near Coates Farm, behind Britwell Hill, SU696912

REFRESHMENTS:
The Goose pub in Britwell Salome provides the only refreshment on the route. It also does good food

ADVICE:
Parking in Britwell Salome is on village roads so take care not to obstruct any entrances or cause bottlenecks. The walk is ten miles without iron ration shops or pubs so take water and a snack. There is a fair amount of rewarding ascending and descending in an attractive part of the west Chilterns

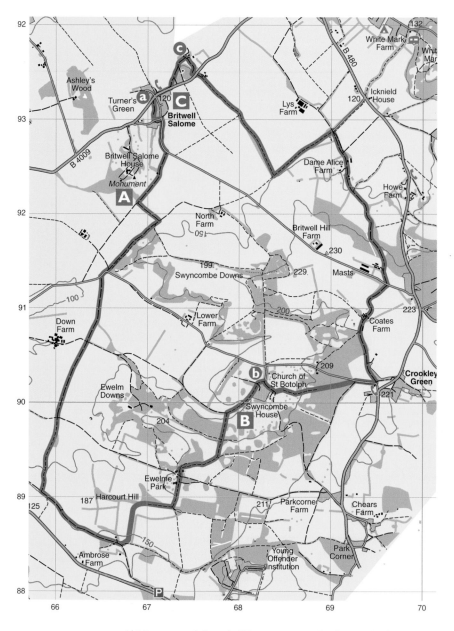

bridleway and Swan's Way sign to walk alongside the parish boundary hedge between Britwell Salome and Ewelme, which follows the classic S-curve of medieval ploughing (see Section **b** of Walk 27). The path leaves the parish boundary, which curves away left, and soon becomes a track past some horse chestnuts. Cross the Ladies Walk track and a field, where you might see pigs in tin bungalows. In the summertime, this is a sort of pig's haven, with pigs dozing in the sun or bathing in their water troughs. The track climbs steadily to the ridge with views of Didcot Power Station, inevitably, and Wittenham Clumps to the right.

The track descends towards a green way ahead. Cross the track onto a footpath beside the field with a hedge on the right, climbing steadily out of the valley, past a wood and then onto the left side of the hedge. The path descends from the ridge of Harcourt Hill. At a T-junction, turn left onto a hedgeless bridleway to descend gently, still on arable land, among knapweed, toadflax, scabious, wild parsnip, St John's wort, red bartsia, nipplewort, dwarf mallow, wild basil and cuckoo pint in berry among other wild summer flowers in the verges, and peacock butterflies in some numbers. Below in the valley bottom is Ambrose Farm with a range of barns converted to houses.

Littleworth Hill. Ewelme's parish boundary hedge

Pass a wood of young beech trees on the right, then a bungalow. Pass dead elms on the left, turn left onto a track and follow it right. I found myself watching comma butterflies on hazel leaves and nettles with a couple of Duke of Burgundy fritillaries dancing in the summer sunlight above my head. At this point one could easily go wrong: ignore the footpath straight on within a hazel, beech and oak belt and go around its left outer edge, soon turning left along the right-hand side of a deep hedge uphill with clustered bellflowers, horehound, white campion, wild basil, black medick, St John's wort, self-heal and red bartsia in the verge and underfoot.

Bear left through the hedge, then right to cross a ploughed field to head straight ahead for a tree gap by a footpath sign. Go right onto a track with a beechwood on the left and a hedge on the right. At a clearing, pick up the Ridgeway Path, turning left onto it and soon skirting the grounds of Ewelme Park, whose gatehouse bellcote has a weathervane dated 1913. Carry straight on to follow the Ridgeway Path; it curves around the edge of a field, then passes through Jacob's Tent woods, mostly beech with some huge poplars and ashes. Through a kissing gate, the path descends through pretty sheep pasture and out via another kissing gate to turn right into a path along the valley bottom lined with lime and horse chestnuts. The path passes Swyncombe House's grounds with some fine specimen trees, almost an arboretum, and through

The track at Harcourthill Shaw

gates at the end of the track to Swyncombe Church where the route leaves the Ridgeway Path.

B   Swyncombe manor and St Botolph's church were held by the abbey of Bec in Normandy from 1086, as were North Stoke and Ipsden (Walk 14). The church is Norman, late 11th Century, with areas of flints laid in the herringbone pattern characteristic of pre-1100 churches. It is three-celled, with a nave, chancel and an apsidal or semi-circular east end and the church survived a restoration by Benjamin Ferrey in the 1850s relatively intact. Nearby are the farmbuildings and stables, with a fox weathervane that conceal Swyncombe House, itself an 1840s replacement for an Elizabethan mansion that burned down. The old rectory is a grander building than the church and dates from 1803, obviously built by a rector of considerable private means.

b   Enter the churchyard keeping to the right of the church and then leave by the south gate, turning left to follow footpath markers across a drive to a kissing gate. Head diagonally right across fine, sheep-cropped parkland pasture to a gate, then look back to the parkland sweeping south-west along the slopes of the hill with woodland on the crest: quite stunningly beautiful. Through a kissing gate enter the woods on the Chiltern Way, and keep straight on along this path. Church wood is mainly a beechwood with felled clearings rich in rosebay willowherb, ash, hazel and silver birch scrub, together with new plantings of oak and ash. At the crest, the woods become mainly beech again, with some oaks, and the path converges a lane that you follow right into Cookley Green.

Just past the gate to Swyncombe Cricket Club turn left onto a tarmac lane which becomes a private road past cottages within a lime and oak avenue, passing Cookley Green Water Tower, a concrete construction now painted grey. Through a beech wood pass Coates Farm, a brick and flint house with

Sheep in Swyncombe Park

weatherboarded and tiled barns. Reaching a road, cross straight over, at 741ft (226m) and the highest point on the walk, onto a metalled track at Woods Farm. At a farmyard, bear right onto a sunken way. Following white painted arrows on trees, descend the Chiltern escarpment through beechwoods with oaks, ash and dogwood along the sunken way margins. It is an excellent sunken way that eventually joins the drive to Dame Alice Farm, a reference to Geoffrey Chaucer's granddaughter, the Countess of Suffolk, who founded Ewelme School and Almshouses in 1437 and rebuilt Ewelme church around 1432.

The sunken way on Britwell Hill

Past the farm, rejoin the Ridgeway Path, turning left to follow it to a bridleway junction where you turn right at the sign 'Britwell Salome 1.5 km, 1m' by an information board telling us that red kites were reintroduced in 1989, breeding for the first time in 1992. The bridleway is within a tree belt of ash, holly, pine, sycamore, thorn, blackthorn, hazel and whitebeam, descending gently towards Britwell. The tree belt narrows to a scrubby hedge margin, then joins a farm track between hedges. In the evening sun, rabbits are everywhere and speckled woods and commas flutter briskly. Past Cooper's Farm you reach the road and turn briefly right before crossing to a footpath sign and over a stile. The path, alongside a sheep net fence, leads to St Nicholas Church, Britwell Salome.

C   Britwell Salome church and rectory are away from the present village centre, which lies along the main Watlington to Benson road. The path goes past the chequer brick gables of the old rectory which has a timber-framed rear wing. The front facing the church is a good Early Georgian one with box sash windows, a pedimented door hood and a moulded eaves cornice. The church was rebuilt in 1867, reusing the Norman nave door, actually for some reason moving it to the chancel.

c From the church walk along the road past a granary and a long range of farmbuildings. At a bend, go right through a gate opposite to a pretty tree-fringed and part watercress-filled pond. Follow the footpath beside a hedge with paddocks on the right and out through a gate to the road. Walk along the road verge to the village and end the walk with a well-earned pint in The Goose pub.

The pond in Britwell Salome

WATLINGTON

This walk starts and finishes in the ancient market town of Watlington with its narrow streets and fine range of Georgian and timber-framed houses radiating from the Restoration period brick Town Hall. From here, the route skirts Pyrton and catches a glimpse of the park to Shirburn Castle before heading for the Ridgeway Path, leaving it to climb to Christmas Common through a spectacular stretch of downland on the edge of a combe. The route returns to Watlington passing Watlington Park.

A Watlington is situated on the old Icknield Way and remains a quiet market town and all the more appealing, apart from the traffic of course. It had a peaceful Victorian era, so was able to hang on to its legacy of timber-framed and Georgian and early 19th-Century buildings, unlike other towns. Although the railway eventually reached Watlington it was only a branch line from Princes Risborough and did not lead to dramatic developments and closed many years ago. At its centre is the Town Hall paid for by Thomas Stonor, which was built in 1665 in a mellow red brick. Originally, the upper floor was used for the grammar school with the market below. Watlington is a remarkably coherent historic town. There are many fine brick fronts and timber-framed buildings, including, in the High Street, the jettied Old Barley Mow. Several grand 18th-Century houses such as Well House and High street House, both with box sashes, testify to Georgian prosperity. There are also some excellent houses in the north-south road, Shirburn Street and, to the south of the High Street junction, Couching Street. At the west end of High Street the road divides into Chapel Street and Church Street. Chapel street includes 17th-Century thatched cottages, including Black Horse Cottage, dating from the 15th-Century and cruck-framed. The church is a disappointment as it was rebuilt in 1877 and only the 15th-Century tower remains.

a From the car park entrance, turn left and walk down Hill Road, cross over the junction into the High Street where you can admire the attractive and well cared for Georgian and timber-framed houses. Bear right into the more cottage-styled Chapel Street, passing the Chequers pub and then Watlington Primary School. Following the rather hidden sign to the Sports Hall car park and skirting the edge of the playing field

MAP:
HARVEY Route Map Ridgeway; OS Landranger Sheets 164, 165 & 175, OS Explorer No 171 Chiltern Hills West

START/FINISH:
Watlington, Hill Road Car-park SU690944. There is a bus service to Watlington from Oxford, No 101. The M1 service from High Wycombe to Reading passes through Watlington

DISTANCE:
8½ miles (13.5 km)

APPROXIMATE TIME:
3 hours

HIGHEST POINT:
787ft (240m) near Christmas Common SU714935

REFRESHMENTS:
Pubs and shops in Watlington. The Fox and Hounds pub in Christmas Common

ADVICE:
A relatively easy walk for navigation with one long climb up to Christmas Common

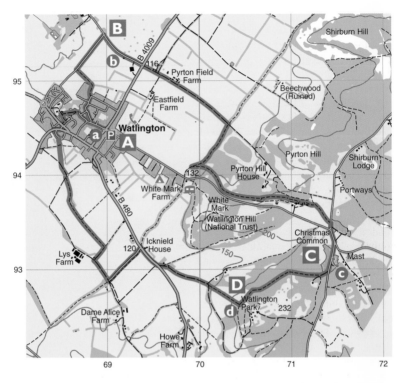

Watlington High Street

with crops on the right, I saw a peregrine falcon hunting the hedges. Right onto the lane, walk to the junction, noting woundwort, lesser burdock, herb robert and hogweed in the hedge in summer. At the T-junction turn right, and the 18th-Century parkland of Shirburn Castle will now be on the left.

B Shirburn Castle is definitely not open to the public, but is a most interesting building. The moated castle was licenced by the King in 1377 and it was built in brick, rather like Herstmonceux in Sussex. It was dramatically altered by the Earls of Macclesfield, who bought the estate in 1716. The grounds, visible from the lane, were laid out around 1720 and made more informally picturesque later in the 18th Century. Alongside the lane are a row of holm oaks and in the park can be seen normal parkland trees including limes, oaks and sweet chestnuts: you may even glimpse the castle's battlements.

b You are now on the Oxfordshire Way, a way-marked route from Henley to Bourton on the Water. Crossing the main road, walk towards the Ridgeway Path, the summer verges bright with a great variety of wild flowers including agrimony, bindweed, wild hops, knapweed, scabious, St John's wort and white campion while meadow browns, gatekeepers and, more unusually, commas gambolled in the sunshine.

Reaching the Ridgeway Path, turn right and follow it to the first stile on the left by the Ridgeway noticeboard. This path can get very overgrown in summer, but I walked back a few yards and cut up through another path to join the correct route, noting a buddleia which was attracting a range of butterflies: clouded yellows, marbled whites, red admirals, painted ladies and commas. Follow yellow arrows uphill through scrubby woodland with some yews and eventually emerge onto more open ground and climb the right hand side of the most wonderful combe for flowers and butterflies. It is parallel to Hill Road and less well known than Watlington Hill, the National Trust land on the other side of the road. To list a few of the more interesting flowers to wet your appetite: common centaury, trefoils, yellow-wort, vetches, ladies bedstraw, wild strawberries, ripe enough to eat, foxgloves and common spotted orchids. Butterflies included commas, Duke of Burgundy fritillaries and marbled whites, and red kites soared in the sky above.

The Orchard, a cottage in Christmas Common

Tearing myself away, I carried on uphill to meet the Oxfordshire Way, emerging onto the road and turning right, past the junction with the Watlington road to follow the road signed 'Cookley Green' and 'Nettlebed'. At a Y junction follow the road round the bend past a phone box into Christmas Common hamlet.

C Christmas common is little more than a line of houses and cottages with a small church, The Nativity, built in 1889 in brick with timber tracery windows and a small belfry, and a pub, The Fox and Hounds. If open, eat and/or sample a pint of Brakspears, brewed in nearby Henley.

An ancient tree in Watlington Park

c With your back to the pub, turn right along the road and then right through gates beside a charming Gothic lodge of about 1800. The walls of End Lodge are painted pink, with Gothic-arched windows and doors. Walk along the drive to Watlington Park and at a clearing the path turns right to follow arrows on trees though what looks like former open parkland, with big oaks and beeches amid smaller trees and scrub. There is extensive Indian balsam before the path enters National Trust woodland, Lower Dean Wood. The wood is now more a Chiltern beechwood. Follow the arrows painted on trees and cross a cleared grassland strip, which gives Watlington Park long views over the Oxfordshire vales and gives the walker a glimpse of the upper storey, pediment and chimneys of the mansion.

D Watlington Park was built for John Tilson who bought the land from the Stonor family in 1758. It is more of a villa than a major country house, square with five windows to each elevation, three windows in pedimented projections and one with the three as a bay window. It is built in brick and is smaller than it was until the 1950s, when a southern range of 1911 was removed to its architectural benefit.

d Immediately across the cleared grass belt, turn right over a stile to descend a grassy down, in summer amid the self-heal, nipplewort, hawksbeard, St John's wort and centaury. Passing through a tree belt, mainly of ash trees, the path joins a track which descends steadily, then past a Neo-Georgian lodge to the road. Turn right and walk along the road as far as the Ridgeway Path junction where you turn left onto it, signed to Lys Mill and Dame Alice Farm. This is a tarmacked section of lane and at a crossroads turn right onto a concrete road and off the Ridgeway Path with a sign to 'Watcombe Manor Farm Partnership'. Past a wheelwash beside the road, there was much mallow along the left verge before reaching a steel gate with a sign nearby stating that there was no public right of way ahead and the footpath to the right. Duly turn right.

The path goes alongside a hedge on the right hand side, then turns left with post and wire fences and between fields to descend gradually towards Watlington, with good views back to the Chiltern escarpment. Passing a willow girt pond, brightly coloured newly hatched tortoiseshell butterflies dried their wings in the sun and flew, while in the trees house martin parents encouraged their fledglings to fly, which they eventually did to my delight.

At a gate further on, turn right to leave the track onto a footpath with a post and wire fence on the left and a hedge, ditch and stream on the right with rose bay willow herb along the hedge margin. Ignoring a footpath to the left, go through a kissing gate and follow the hedge round to the left, then through another kissing gate onto a track which becomes a tarmac lane, The Goggs, and passes Thatchers Cottage to the road. Now in Watlington, cross the road onto a path, then right into a lane of modern houses, Hurdlers Green, and out to the main road, Cuxham Road, the B480. Turn left here and at a sign to Pyrton and the Church turn right. If the Church is no longer closed for remedial work (as was the case in February 2001), take a right fork by a cul-de-sac sign to visit the medieval tower. Continue along the lane past the church hall and turn left at the footpath T-junction to re-enter the High Street and then back to the car park.

Watlington Park house

A SCULPTURE TRAIL IN THE WOODS STOKENCHURCH

MAPS:
HARVEY Route Map Ridgeway; OS Landranger Sheets 165, 175, OS Explorer No 171 Chiltern Hills West

START/FINISH:
Cowleaze Car Park (follow signs to Chiltern Sculpture Trail) SU725956. There are no buses to Cowleaze Wood; the walk could be started from Stokenchurch, which is served by several bus routes

DISTANCE:
10 miles (16km)

APPROXIMATE TIME:
4 hours

HIGHEST POINT:
843ft (257m) Cowleaze Wood spot height

REFRESHMENTS:
Several pubs exist in Stokenchurch plus Del Boy's Stores for iron rations, a bakery and a fish and chip shop. I lunched in the Fleur de Lis pub, but the King's Arms, The Four Horseshoes and the Royal Oak (in Church Street) are also close to the route. Just off the Ridgeway Path, Hill Farm does teas and refreshments on Saturdays, Sundays and Bank Holiday Mondays

ADVICE:
Some sections of the walk can be very muddy. Allow time – an hour or so – to walk round the Sculpture Trail in Cowleaze Woods

Cowleaze Wood has been the location of the Chiltern Sculpture Trail since it was opened in 1990. It is managed by the Chiltern Sculpture Trust and the Forestry Commission who have created a waymarked trail through the woods with over 20 sculptures near or off the path. There is a post with the title of the piece, its date and the name of the sculptor. Some are easy to locate, such as Fred Baier's brightly coloured steel benches near the start of the trail or No 8, Jon Mill's 'Bell Tower'. Others are difficult to spot, including No 21, Anya Gallacio's carpet laid in the woods with a tree through part of it and No 18, Andrew Sabin's 'Above and Below', which consists of black bands painted on trees. It is a most enjoyable experience even if some pieces are a little obvious, such as No 15, Laura Ford's 'Nature Girl', a 1993 bronze of a section of tree trunk carried on a girl's feet, while others are more humerous, such as No 3, Paul Amey's 'Fish Tree' of 1990. For the purposes of the walk, however, the last sculpture you see should be No 16, Richard La Trobe 'Bateman's Bench' of 1993, which is near the eastern end of the wood by the point where the walk route leaves Cowleaze Wood. This is a double tripod, the upper supporting the lower with its benches by means of wires. It is about 20ft (6m) high, so should not be too easy to miss.

a For those with limited time, or who wish to leave the Sculpture Trail until the end, the public footpath through the wood starts at the opposite (southern) end of the car park from the trail. Follow white arrows to join a broader track. After a path junction, the route passes sculptures 8 and 9 and leaves the wood into the Wormsley Estate, as a notice board informs you, having just passed Richard Bateman's *Bench*. You emerge into a beautiful valley and descend through a field with well-wooded slopes opposite. Briefly left along the valley bottom lane, its banks in summer rich in marjoram, climb a stile right into green pasture, then skirt Lower Vicars Farm, a flint and brick Chiltern farmhouse with a mellow tiled roof, before climbing out of the valley into beechwoods where speckled woods danced in the sunshine and delicate blue harebells and purple clustered bellflowers abound. At a footpath junction near the top of the hill turn right, still in the beechwood but with oaks and some hazel coppice. I disturbed a muntjak deer, while marbled white and gatekeeper

The Chiltern Sculpture Trail in Cowleaze Wood: John Mill's 'Bell Tower'

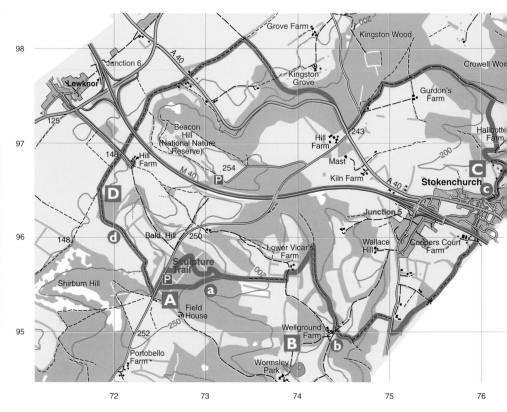

butterflies flew in the clearings. The track descended to a road, the drive to Wormsley House. On the right is Wellground Farm, one of the Wormsley Estate farms.

B The Wormsley Park was bought in the early 1980s by Sir John Paul Getty II in a somewhat run down state from the Fane family who had transformed the 16th- and 17th-Century house in the earlier 18th Century and stuccoed it around 1800. Set in a remarkably secluded valley the house offers great privacy, but the cricket-loving owner has also built a superb thatched cricket pavilion and pitch in the grounds and has also created, in effect, an 18th-Century English Picturesque park of which Capability Brown himself would not be ashamed. The farms and farmbuildings have also benefited from full restoration, as has the landscape, including the beechwoods and the farmland. Sir John was also instrumental in the highly successful introduction of the Spanish red kite into the Chilterns where it has proved remarkably successful.

b Cross the drive and follow the path uphill through woods, bearing left at a track junction and guided by white arrows painted on trees. In places it is possible to glimpse Wormsley House down the valley behind you. The final section before the road is often very muddy. At the road, turn right for about 100 yards (91m) before turning left along a track, then left again after about 50 yards (46m) to follow arrows through the woods. Leaving the woods over a stile by a cottage, cross a series of fields and a series of stiles, with fences on the left and at one point a splendid view down the famously beautiful Hambleden Valley towards Fingest. At Coopers Court Farm, now on the Chiltern Way, bear right across a field to a stile close to the entrance to a Ctesiphon arch section tunnel under the roaring M40, which leads into Stokenchurch where there is a choice of pubs. I chose the Fleur de Lis and lunched there.

The Chiltern Sculpture Trail in Cowleaze Wood: Richard Le Trobe Bateman's 'Bench' of 1993

c For nearly 1,000 years, Wormsley Park and Stokenchurch had been in Oxfordshire, but were transferred to Buckinghamshire in 1895. Until the 1960s, Stokenchurch was a village on the main London to Oxford Road with a coaching inn, the Kings Arms, and built around a number of greens, some now with splendid large lime trees. However, the

An entrance to Aston Rowant
National Nature Reserve form
the Ridgeway Path

development of the M40 transformed the village, with housing estates springing up between the village and the motorway and along the Ibstone road. To the walker, however, it offers a great choice of refreshment.

c   Cross the A40 at the pelican crossing, turn left onto the pavement in front of the King's Arms Hotel and turn right into Church Street. The mediaeval parish church is on the north side of the village, off Church Street, its churchyard entered by a recently well-restored Victorian lych gate. From the peaceful churchyard northwards lies open country, while the pebble-dashed church is crowned by a shingled bell turret which is supposed to have a Norman core. From the churchyard walk east along Church Street and left down Park Lane, just beyond the Royal Oak pub. Continue down the lane, passing the road to Longburrow Hall on the left and a footpath on the right. Note the extensive Indian balsam and rose bay willow herb, while passing the gatepiers to Mallards Court. Beyond this as the track begins to bear right, turn left on a path with a shed on the right and bear left across a rough field to enter a beech hanger. About 50 yards (46m) after a kissing gate, turn sharp right, downhill, at a path junction to reach a hairpin bend in a metalled road. In about 25 yards (23m), climb a stile to go left across pasture. This is a most pretty valley, but at the bottom cross into a field, the path heading uphill, then into Lott Wood, a beech hanger or 'hanging wood' with the occasional odour of stinkhorns, to descend into a dry valley within the woods.

Cross a track and at a footpath T-junction, turn left to walk along the valley floor, climbing gradually. At a three-way footpath junction, bear left and later turn left beyond a field on the left, eventually emerging from High Wood near a brick and flint cottage, shortly to join a track and, shortly, a metalled road. Turn left at the road and head for the Telecom Tower, built in 1960 and a landmark for miles around. Turn right along the A40 on a path within the verge and, just before a chevron bend marker, leave the road right to a wide track that descends the escarpment through Aston Woods, signposted 'Bridleway Aston Rowant'. This is good beechwood interspersed with ash, wild cherry and a few oaks, whitebeam, sycamore and hornbeam and much holly and thorn scrub as an understorey. The track descends, and at a footpath arrow go right just before a 'No Riding' sign. The slope now descends steeply off the escarpment, the path still in a holloway, eventually emerging into a hedged, green lane with much ribbed melilot and new-hatched tortoiseshells glowing in the sun.

At the Ridgeway Path turn left, here you will find a section of the Icknield Way ancient trackway. Across the A40 the Path climbs gradually to skirt Beacon Hill, the eastern part of Aston Rowant National Nature Reserve and you pass its kissing gate access. On the margins there is meadow cranesbill and soon you pass under the M40. At the first crossroads beyond the M40 I was delighted to see a sign advertising tea and cakes, as I was distinctly parched on a hot summer's day. I turned left to

Approaching the M40 bridge on the Ridgeway Path

A most welcome sight: Hill Farm's teas

Hill Farm, a 150-yard (137m) diversion, for a cup of tea on the farmhouse lawn.

Alternatively, those who started the walk at Stkenchurch, might wish to make the detour to Lewknor from this point. Turn right on a quiet metalled road for about 700 yards (640m), cross a main road and go down steps from a lay-by slightly to the left to follow a lane for a further 200 yards (183m) to the village centre. Ye Olde Leathern Bottel is almost opposite.

Back on the Ridgeway Path, continue south-west, the track wide between low hedges with a good range of wild flowers in summer including melilot, trefoils and vetches. In 500 yards (457m) at the second footpath sign, turn left, diagonally right across a field and into a scrubby wood of thorn, sycamore, spindle and birch. This is Old Cricketground Plantation and part of the Aston Rowant National Nature Reserve.

D   Aston Rowant National Nature Reserve, a registered Site of Special Scientific Interest and first notified in 1973, covers over 300 acres on both sides of the M40. It is one of the largest surviving complexes in the Chilterns of beech woodland, mixed scrub and juniper and chalk grassland.

d   Out of the Plantation the footpath bears left to climb alongside the Nature Reserve, initially past beech with spindle, birch and hornbeam, then past lush chalk grassland on the slopes of Bald Hill. At various times of year orchids can be found here, including butterfly, bee, frog, common spotted, pyramidal and early purple, and the rare Chiltern gentian. I stayed outside the reserve and followed the fence, then soon after a right-hand bend, turned left along a steep path, initially between hedges, back in the Nature Reserve, and reached the road. Crossing this and, now within Cowleaze Wood, you turn left to follow the track which runs parallel and about 15–20 yards (14m) from the Christmas Common road back to the start.

BLEDLOW AND RADNAGE

This route descends from the hills above Chinnor to the historic village of Bledlow on the spring line at the foot of the Chilterns, while at its southernmost point is the scattered settlement of Radnage with its outstanding church. Along the way are some of the area's finest historic woodlands and rich wild flower habitats, such as the slopes of Lodge Hill

A The walk starts in the car park to the Chinnor Hill Nature Reserve managed by the Berkshire, Buckinghamshire and Oxfordshire Wildlife Trust, a reserve noted for its orchids. From here the walk passes through Bledlow Great Wood, a large ancient woodland, partly a 'hanging' beechwood on the escarpment with the rest on the plateau top, a total of 120 acres. At various times of year one would hope to see such exotic plants as yellow-bird's nest, white helleborine, narrow lipped helleborine, sanicle, dog's mercury and bird's nest orchids.

MAPS:
OS Landranger Sheet 165,
OS Explorer No 181 Chiltern
Hills North & No 171
Chiltern Hills West

START/FINISH:
Chinnor Hill Nature Reserve
Car-park SP766002. The 331
bus route from Thame to
High Wycombe could drop
you off at the corner of Hill
Top Lane. The bus is every 2
hours, the last bus at 1800
and not on Sundays

DISTANCE:
9 miles (14km)

APPROXIMATE TIME:
3½ hours

HIGHEST POINT:
820ft (250m) at the starting
point

REFRESHMENTS:
The Lions at Bledlow pub at
about 2 miles (3km)

ADVICE:
There are no refreshments
on the route apart from the
well-known pub in Bledlow
so carry water and whatever
else you need, particularly if
the weather is hot. The route
does a fair amount of
ascents and descents, both
off and back up the
escarpment as well as hills
and valleys in the southern
part of the route

Approaching the Lions of Bledlow pub

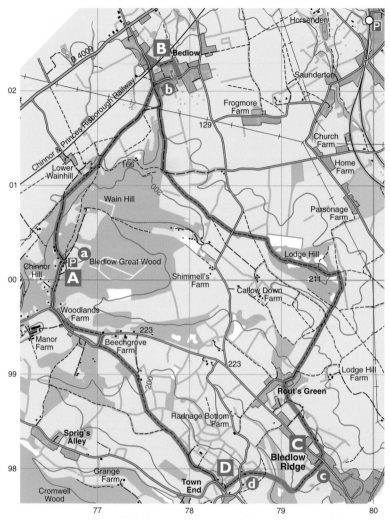

a From the car park go left of the information sign on a tarmac drive, then past an aptly named cottage, Windy Ridge, where the path descends steeply in woodland down a fine sunken way. There are many yew trees amid the beeches, also ash and cherries. At the Ridgeway Path turn right to a fairly level section on the Icknield Way, with some hazel coppicing and thorn and maple scrub, and a variety of wild flowers including violet-blue nettle-leaved bellflowers and lighter blue harebells. Having passed between garden fences (ignore the bridleway on the right then left) the route leaves the Ridgeway Path for a while. It passes beside a brick cottage, through a

Mellow roof tiles on an early
17th century house in Bledlow

gate and left onto the Swan's Way bridleway to descend along
a metalled track, lined with lady's bedstraw, pink and white
bindweed flowers, field forget-me-nots, hedge bedstraw,
scabious, knapweed, sheep's bit, dog roses, cuckoo pint in
berry, and wild hops festooning the thorn hedges. Where the
track bends right, bear left onto the path cut through crops,
aiming at the white walls and tiled roofs of the Lions of
Bledlow pub.

B   Bledlow village has as its main street Church End, which
runs east from the Lions of Bledlow with a number of good,
early 17th-Century timber-framed cottages, mostly with
herringbone or coursed brick infill between the timbers, some
of the brick being as old as 1700, then Holy Trinity parish
church. This has Norman fragments and a nave arcade of
about 1200, the west tower being late 13th Century. Within is
an 'Aylesbury' font, one of a group of Norman fonts that look
like chalices with fluted bowls: there are two more on these
walks further east in the Chilterns at Monks Risborough and
Great Kimble (Walk 22). The church is among the best
medieval examples in Buckinghamshire and has recently had
its medieval and later wall paintings restored. Immediately
east of the church is The Lyde Garden, a deep ravine from
which the Lyde stream emerges. It has been landscaped by
Lord Carrington as a water garden with exotic plants, timber
walkways and bridges. Beyond lies an interesting group of
modern brick houses, built in 1975 by Aldington, Craig and
Collinge, as with the Lyde Garden, for villagers and built by
Lord Carrington who lives at the Manor House, a good
Georgian house on the south side of the lane.

Wain Hill from near the Lions of Bledlow pub

b From the Lions of Bledlow walk down West Lane and under the railway bridge, now used by a preservation railway, the Princes Risborough and Chinnor Railway, which runs steam and diesel trains. Opposite Westfield Farm, turn right through a hedge and over a stile, then diagonally across pasture to cross the railway, another short pasture and a stile and left along a metalled track and at a cottage right up a path, which runs alongside The Lyde with the churchyard on the right. After visiting the church, walk back west along the road to the Lions of Bledlow, where you turn left along the track south up to the Ridgeway Path.

Follow the Ridgeway Path which turns right at a kissing gate almost immediately to walk through sheep cropped pasture with views of Whiteleaf Cross (Walk 22) and a field of borage on the left. Crossing the road head for Lodge Hill, a solitary hill rising over 100ft (30.5m) above its surroundings. At its foot is a lush meadow with many wild flowers such as horehound, marjoram and St John's wort. Then the path ascends quite steeply and passes through beechwood and clearings and scrubby downland, again with huge variety of wild flowers in summer, including great mullein, pyramidal orchids, clustered bellflowers, stonecrop, meadow saxifrage, agrimony, birds foot trefoil, harebells, wild basil, betony and scabious. Descend the hill and as you near the bottom, go through a kissing gate, turn right off the Ridgeway Path onto a bridleway. Whilst looking for Red Kites, which now frequent the area, follow the track across a valley and up the other side and at the top, to the left of corrugated iron farmbuildings, going through a gate onto a metalled track which became a metalled lane. This is Routs Green and near the entrance to Firs Lodge turn left onto a path, initially between gardens. This is the Chiltern Way and follow its waymarks through pastures with some good views left, then a gravelled drive which leads to Chinnor Road, the main road through Bledlow Ridge.

C   Until this Century, Bledlow Ridge was a sparse settlement with a string of farms and a few labourers cottages. Bledlow was one of those classic narrow Chiltern parishes with the village centre and the village's medieval open fields in the vale north of the Chiltern escarpment with hill pasture, woodland and commons or heaths in a long strip extending onto the plateau. Bledlow Ridge lies along the ridge above two deep valleys either side and this elevated healthy position has proved attractive so there are many modern houses to fill in the gaps and take advantage of the spectacular views from both sides of the ridge. The church of St Paul, rebuilt in 1868, replaced a chapel of ease to Bledlow church, itself three miles away, to serve the uphill parishioners.

c   Across Chinnor Road, taking the path beside Yewsden Cottage, clear of the houses the views across the Radnage valley are superb. The path bears right in a wood and you ignore a path continuing straight on. Beyond the wood over a stile, cross exceptionally rich chalk grassland noted for its bee, pyramidal and fragrant orchids – although I did not spot any. Descend steeply and at the lowest point, cross a stile ahead to a stile, ignoring a path to the left. Eventually you reach and cross a series of horse paddocks and stiles to the churchyard of St Mary, Radnage.

Lodge Hill from near Wain Hill

The porch at St Mary's Church, Radnage

D St Mary's Church, Radnage, sits on the side of its valley with only the Georgian former rectory for company and a timber-framed cottage a little further down the lane. Radnage is a very scattered series of ends or hamlets with no real village centre. It is most picturesquely situated and was built about 1200, consisting of a central tower, chancel and nave. It is distinctly wasp-waisted as the tower is narrower than either the chancel or the nave. Apart from some 14th- and 15th-Century windows and shallower, pitched late-medieval roofs, the church has an unusual homogeneity and has been little altered. Presumably the population it served did not grow sufficiently to necessitate adding aisles. It is dominated, as are distant views, by the large central tower.

d From the churchyard head to the road and, crossing it, climb a stile into a field. Walk up the length of this narrowish pasture, over a stile onto the drive to Kirk Stile. Reaching the road turn right and past Whites Farm leave the road, turning right onto a tarmacked track, signed to Daws Hill Farm, with a large wheat field on the left. Where the farm drive swings right, carry straight on up a green lane which climbs gradually and can be very muddy. When the track curves left leave it at a stile marked RA4 by the Chiltern Society. Follow the path across the pasture in the base of the dry valley, over a stile, and climb steeply uphill to the left of a thick ash and hawthorn hedge with dog roses in summer. The track then goes through the edge of a hanging beechwood with holly and bramble undergrowth. Out of the woods and over a stile, walk along the left side of a hedge, with a view to the left of the Telecom Tower at Stokenchurch. Leaving the fields by a stile, turn right onto the road and, at the bend, go left to leave the road. Cross the stile and head along a grass track towards modern farmbuildings – stay with the footpath between them. Beyond these you reach the road and, taking care, turn right into Hill Top Lane to walk back to the car park with beechwoods either side interspersed with ash, sycamore and cherry trees and a number of cottages.

PRINCES RISBOROUGH

The second walk, situated entirely in the Buckinghamshire Chilterns, is focused on the attractive market town of Princes Risborough, a town whose manor was held in the 14th Century by the warrior Black Prince and where his royal horse stud was located. The walk passes through the vale hamlets of Horsenden and Saunderton on its way back to the Chilterns, climbing to Loosley Row, where Samuel Palmer painted a view which included the 17th-Century Lacey Green Windmill, also featured on the route. The later stage of the walk goes through delightful Chiltern beechwoods before descending steeply back to the town.

A The Ridgeway Path descends from the hills towards Princes Risborough, a delightful Buckinghamshire market town, again partly utilising the ancient Icknield Way track. This gives the long distance walker a chance to replenish supplies very close to the Path. For us, the town provides the starting point for walk Number 21.

Although much expanded with housing estates to the west, south and east, the historic core is intact and the fine Edwardian spire of the medieval parish church can be seen from many viewpoints along the Path. The High Street, now by-passed by the Aylesbury to High Wycombe main road has all the appearance of a medieval planned market town, many of the buildings concealing late-medieval and 17th-Century timber-frames.

At the junction of High Street, Duke Street and Church Street, the brick and slate Market House crowned by a clock cupola, was built in 1824, with the town council chamber in the upper room over the open arcaded ground floor where the Women's Institute often sell excellent home-made cakes. Needless to say, Church Street leads to the parish church and a less urban part of the town. The Manor House, now owned by the National Trust, is a mellow brick house of the early 17th Century, with a hipped old tile roof.

To the west of the churchyard is a car park called The Mount. This unprepossessing space is in fact of considerable historic interest, for beneath the dreary tarmac are the foundations of the manor house, excavated in 1955, of the Edward, the Black

MAPS:
HARVEY Route Map
Ridgeway; OS Landranger
Sheet 165, OS Explorer No
181 Chiltern Hills North

START/FINISH:
The Mount Car Park, Church
Street, Princes Risborough, in
the town centre SP805034.
Princes Risborough is served
by several bus routes
including the 323 and 324,
and a minor adjustment to
the route gives access from
the railway station (Chiltern
Line)

DISTANCE:
8 miles (13km)

APPROXIMATE TIME:
3 hours

HIGHEST POINT:
About 775ft (236m) near
Parslow's Hillock SP829021

REFRESHMENTS:
Plentiful in Princes
Risborough and at The Whip
Inn in Lacey Green, near the
Windmill about half way
round the route

ADVICE:
An easy walk for navigation
with a steepish climb up to
Lacey Green and a short
sharp descent to Brimmers
Farm

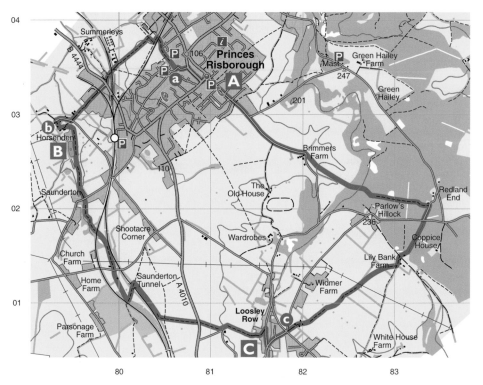

Prince, the victor of the Battle of Crecy and a brilliant military commander during the Hundred Years' War. He was the eldest son of Edward III and died in 1376, having been granted the manor by his father in 1343. By 1543 the town was known as Princes Risborough to distinguish it from nearby Monks or east Risborough, which is on Walk 22. The manor was the site of a royal stud farm whose buildings have not been found and its moated site circled the churchyard to the north to cross Church Lane and include the now converted barns. To the west of The Mount car park, was a royal hunting park, now built over.

The town received a weekly market charter in 1523, but expanded little even when the railway arrived in 1862 until the 20th-Century expansion, which also brought the flamboyant sub-Byzantine Roman Catholic church of St Theresa, built in 1937 and with a huge, brick dome.

a From The Mount car park, visit the parish church to the east, then turn left down an unmade road, Church Lane, with the Manor House on the opposite side. Continue past some converted barns on the right and Monks Staithe on the left. This is a timber-framed cottage with a circular stone chimney which was rented by the aviatrix, Amy Johnson, in the 1930s. When the path divides, continue straight on along the lesser path beside the stream to a bridge over the railway. Immediately after crossing the railway, turn left and follow the path round a right-hand bend beside fencing to a junction. Now turn left again and follow the clear path across a field to a bridge under a railway, emerging by Park Mill, a former watermill and now two houses. Crossing the main road, walk straight through the Princes industrial estate, leaving it over a stile to head for Horsenden through a field where orange tip butterflies and hawthorn flies make the most of any warm sunshine.

B Horsenden is a pretty and remote hamlet with a small parish church and manor house, its lane overhung by tall horse chestnut and lime trees. The 15th Century church is in fact a fragment, the nave having been demolished in 1765 and the stone used to build the tower. The churchyard is delightful and gives views into the grounds of Horsenden Manor, a Regency stucco house of about 1810 incorporating parts of both a 15th-Century moated manor house and a Georgian house with battlements. The older house had been garrisoned for the King during the Civil War by Sir John Denham in the midst of hostile Parliamentarian territory.

Princes Risborough Manor House

Immediately south of Horsenden, in Roundabout Wood, is a deserted medieval village site, which includes a moated manor house. Two miles into the walk the route diverts to the medieval St Mary's Church in Saunderton, with the moat of the former medieval manor house of the de Saunderton family in a well-wooded site with alder trees and poplars.

b Retrace your steps east from Horsenden church past the

Park Mill House, near Princes Risborough

gates to the Manor House. Climb a stile to walk through meadows with occasional parkland trees, limes and horse chestnuts. Alongside the Manor House grounds, largely hidden from view, pass some lakes, while overhead red kites wheel and crows caw in Roundabout Wood with its dried-up medieval moat. Heading south, cross a road emerging from between gardens into a field and a little way along it divert right to Saunderton Church, passing a moated manor site known nowadays as Saunderton Marsh, noting beside the path a lot of greater horsetail plants. Back on the path the route crosses the railway via two stiles and then continues through pasture, submerged by meadow thistles with hedges of mayflower and blackthorn in flower. Across a road the path goes briefly through the grounds of The Old Rectory, an attractive late Georgian house with an elegant Tuscan columned porch. A stile leads into old sheep-cropped pastures with numerous brimstone butterflies. You descend to turn left onto the Ridgeway Path, back north across the railway, which here emerges from the Saunderton Tunnel into a deep cutting. Through a kissing gate, turn right to leave the Ridgeway Path and walk alongside the railway cutting, with arable land to your left. The path leaves the railway to head south-east, to cross the main road and head for Loosley Row. It briefly meets a lane and then climbs out of the valley, up to the hamlet, past farmbuildings of Collins Farm on the left. Unfortunately, these are modern replacements for the thatched barns painted by Samuel Palmer who stayed here in 1845, depicting one view looking downhill towards Lodge Hill, the other uphill towards Lacey Green Windmill. Reaching the road turn right, then left up Loosley Hill to The Whip Inn at the crossroads, a most welcome halt for refreshment.

C   Behind The Whip Inn is Lacey Green Windmill, which was superbly restored in the 1970s by the Chiltern Society and is open between May and September on Sundays and Bank Holiday afternoons. It is a smock mill of about 1650, clad in modern, stained weatherboarding with white sails. Apparently moved here from Chesham in 1821, it occasionally grinds corn. Further north-east, from Lily Bank Farm to Redland End, the route follows Grim's Ditch for half a mile (0.8kms), that great Iron Age boundary earthwork discussed in more detail in Walk 24.

c   Refreshed, I left The Whip Inn and beyond the lane to the windmill. I climbed a stile, onto The Chiltern Way waymarked path into pasture to walk past the Windmill and cross a shallow valley through a vast field. From here, move through 'horseyculture' paddocks, leaving the last paddock over a stile into a tree-lined sunken way, actually on the course of Grim's Ditch. Beyond the brick,

Lacey Green Windmill

weatherboard and slate farmbuildings of Lily Bank Farm and across Lily Bottom Lane, which is still on the Chiltern Way, walk through beech and conifer woods on a much horse-churned bridleway alongside Grim's Ditch, here parallel earth banks to the left of the path. Navigate by following the normal way marking in Chiltern woodland: a white painted arrow at intervals on tree trunks and I kept my eyes skinned for foxes and muntjac deer which abound hereabouts.

At the road continue straight on, then turn back over a stile into the woods just before the houses of Redland End, with a footpath sign 'Circular Walk'. These woods are mostly beech and conifers, although there are some oaks and a holly undergrowth, but there are virtually no bluebells. Follow the white arrows on trees and occasional marker posts generally in a west-north-west direction. There was some gorse in bright yellow flower, silver birch scrub and occasional sun-lit clearings. Ignore all turnings to left and right while at a footpath crossroads climb a stile and continue straight on, the path now beginning to descend with the beech trees interspersed with old coppice hazel and a few juniper trees. Sun spurge is abundant here and the path soon descends increasingly steeply, some of it with wooden steps. The path emerges over a stile from the woods, having descended about 260ft (80m) in 300 yards (274m) into a great grass meadowed dry valley. The path reaches the road at Brimmers Farm, a typical Chiltern flint and brick farmhouse with weatherboarded farmbuildings. Follow the road north-west back into Princes Risborough, crossing the Ridgeway Path on the southern outskirts as it follows the Icknield Way. At the roundabout turn left, then immediately right into the High Street, left at the Market House into Church Street and back to the car park.

A splash of yellow: oilseed rape east of Loosley Row

MONKS RISBOROUGH AND WHITELEAF CROSS

Although a walk of only 5 miles, this route packs in four small villages of great charm, including Monks Risborough whose Burton Lane cottages are much photographed. Whiteleaf village is at the base of the Chiltern scarp and, from the distant views, is dominated by the Whiteleaf Cross, a cross cut in the chalk.

A The walk starts in the Whiteleaf Hill Car Park and the Cross is the first feature of the walk, although you can see the total picture better from below. It consists of a chalk cut figure of a cross standing on a pyramidal base, although erosion has steadily broadened the base. That is about as far as one can go in deciding what it is all about, for the first known reference of it was in 1742. Current archaeological thinking veers between a 10th-Century commemoration of a nearby battle against the Danes, a medieval figure cut by the lord of the manor, a prehistoric monument subsequently Christianised into a cross shape, or a 17th-Century one, cut as a form of outdoor poor relief.

It stretches downhill from a clearing and the bare hilltop gives wonderful views over the Vale of Aylesbury and south-west

MAP:
HARVEY Route Map Ridgeway; OS Landranger Sheet 165, OS Explorer No 181 Chiltern Hills North

START/FINISH:
Whiteleaf Hill Car Park SP823035. There are no bus routes to this car park, but the 323 and 324 buses between Aylesbury and High Wycombe stop in Monks Risborough, Askett and Great Kimble so the walk could easily be modified to start in any of these three villages

DISTANCE:
5 miles (8km)

APPROXIMATE TIME:
2½ hours

HIGHEST POINT:
About 803ft (245m) Start of the walk in the car park

REFRESHMENTS:
The Plough at Cadsden, The Bernard Arms in Great Kimble, The Three Crowns in Askett and The Red Lion in Whiteleaf, depending on the time of day

ADVICE:
A straightforward walk with a stiff climb at the end back up the Chiltern scarp to the car park. However, it can be very muddy in winter

Princes Risborough from Whiteleaf Hill

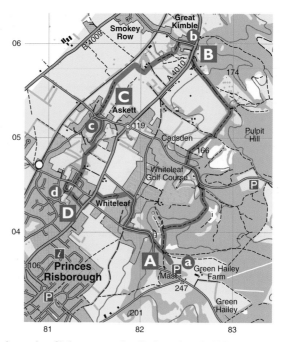

along the Chilterns to the Stokenchurch Telecom tower and the ubiquitous Didcot power station cooling towers beyond. Nearby is a mound surrounded by a low wattle fence and this is an archaeological remain of considerable importance. It is Buckinghamshire's only known and surviving Neolithic earthwork. It is a burial mound surrounded by a shallow ditch and dates from around 2500 BC, a timber burial chamber was found in its centre in excavations in the 1930s.

a Start in the car park with its picnic tables and head for the Chiltern Woodlands information board. Beyond, follow a metalled path into the woods, mostly beech, ash and hazel with some recently planted oaks to merge with the Ridgeway Path. Through a gate, you reach the clearing with the burial mound on the left and the Whiteleaf Cross beyond. After admiring the long views over the lowlands follow the Ridgeway Path descending through woodland with occasional clearings, again mainly beech, ash and the occasional hawthorn. Periwinkles and herb robert flowers line the path in summer and it winds downhill through cleared woodland, dense beech woods and occasional clearings while six-spot burnet moths and meadow brown and ringlet butterflies dart about. Pass the Plough pub and cottages on your left, continue to the end of the lane where it joins the road. Traffic is quite fast on this road and there is no pavement. Cross the road and continue downhill for about 200 yards (183m). The Ridgeway path is the second path on the right and runs between houses. The Path heads towards Pulpit Hill with expansive views to the left over the Vale of Aylesbury and to the right over open downland with hawthorn scrub and woodland beyond.

Continue along the Ridgeway Path, passing the deep combe of The Butts, presumably once used for archery practice, with 'horsey culture' fields on the left. Above the Butts is Pulpit Hill which amid the trees has a well-preserved Iron Age hill fort. Near the path there are a lot of beautiful delicately coloured pink and white dog roses in flower in June, twining over thornbushes and hedges and lady's bedstraw amid the grass. Through a kissing gate, having climbed out of The Butts, turn left onto the North Bucks Way, leaving the Ridgeway Path, to follow the track downhill between unkempt hedges with occasional beeches, sycamores and ashes as standards, turning right at the main road to visit Great Kimble church (if open).

Sheep graze the earthworks at Great Kimble

A thatched cottage in Askett Lane

B Great Kimble Church is noted for its fine Norman font of the 'Aylesbury' type which is rather like a chalice with fluted sides on an ornate base. To the west of the village in the fields is a moated site, medieval fishpond and the earthworks of settlement remains, amid the sheep pasture and probably the site of Great Kimble manor.

b From Great Kimble church turn left down Church Lane, past flint and brick cottages, and left over a stile past a 30 MPH sign onto the footpath to Askett. Passing the willow-fringed medieval fishpond, cross a stream and pass into the earthworks overlain by sheep pasture. The path passes south of the Old Grange, crossing its drive. The grange is a medieval house, much enlarged and very picturesque with an attractive range of old tiled and weatherboarded barns and outbuildings, all set within another moat. Skirt the west arm of the moat, after which there is a choice of paths. Take the one going sharp left towards the railway before turning left to walk roughly parallel to it, then veering away to cross medieval ridge and furrow south of a group of converted barns, keeping to the left of them but hugging their fences in order not to miss a corridor and a double stile at the end. Take the right hand path which takes you to a stile in a corner by a brick wall. The path leads between gardens to the road and Askett village. This was a proper medieval Midland landscape with the sheep grazing the corrugated ridge and furrow fields.

C Askett's curious name derives from East Cot, that is a hamlet at the east edge of Monks Risborough parish. By 1300 there was a manor house, its later 15th-Century hall now rebuilt is found in nearby Meadle. The village was a centre of pillow lace-making and Aylesbury duck breeding and there are some good timber-framed cottages in its lanes.

c   Turn left from the path onto the road through the village, passing the thatch-roofed The Old Barn on the left, now a house. If thirsty, the Three Crowns pub will meet your needs. Turn right at the thatched and timber-framed Askett Farm into Askett Lane, a winding quiet backwater away from the through traffic. There are several more 17th-Century timber-framed cottages along the lane and a large paddock on the right. At the end of the lane is Meadowcroft Farm where you bear left onto a footpath alongside an old mellow brick wall. Crossing a stream turn right immediately to continue alongside the wall, through a sycamore copse and out over a stile into buttercup-covered paddocks, grazed by ponies. Over a stile in the corner of a field, across a stream and along a nettly path to skirt the modern hall of the Whiteleaf Scout Group, you reach Monks Risborough.

Buttercups near Askett

D   Monks Risborough is now joined to Princes Risborough by modern housing estates, but around the superb parish church of St Dunstan its village centre is intact with a park to separate it from the housing. In the park is a 16th-Century dovecote in chalk stone with a tiled pyramid roof and east of the church is the Old Rectory built in 1670 and enlarged in Gothic style in 1863. The church, like Great Kimble, has an 'Aylesbury' font and the village is named Monks Risborough as the manor was held by the monks of Christchurch Priory in Canterbury well before the Norman Conquest of 1066. The parish originally was a long narrow one, a classic chalk hill country one with land in the valley and on the downs, and a charter of AD 903 survives, giving its boundaries, many features of which are still recognisable today. It is a very early charter and, incidentally, contains the first-known reference to the Icknield Way which passes through the parish at Whiteleaf.

Whiteleaf village is strung out along the Icknield Way and its name is a corruption of 'white cliff', which refers to the chalk hills behind and first

A cottage in Whiteleaf

occurs in 1540. There are two groups of timber-framed cottages at each end of the village with the Victorian Whiteleaf House between them set in good grounds. There is also The Red Lion pub for refreshment.

d From the church, walk to Burton Lane with its well-known row of thatched cottages and a timber-framed one named '1590 AD'. The village continues along the main Aylesbury Road with an old forge on the corner. Turn left to cross the road at traffic lights to the Victorian brick and flint school built in 1855 with the former schoolmaster's house to its right. Immediately past the school go through a kissing gate to walk alongside the school fence, then diagonally through pasture with a kestrel hovering overhead towards a tree belt of horse chestnuts and sycamores. A path between iron park fences led to a road, The Holloway, where you turn right up into Whiteleaf village.

Turn right to walk through the village, then left at the end at the junction with Peter's Lane to walk up the hill towards Whiteleaf Cross. At the start of the bend ignore a path to the left and continue past the base of the Cross to a footpath sign. Leave the road to the left to climb very steeply back uphill to the Ridgeway Path. Reaching the Path turn right, soon leaving it to turn left and back to the car park.

BEACON HILL AND CHEQUERS

This 5½ mile walk circles around Chequers, the weekend retreat of Prime Ministers since 1921. It starts at Coombe Hill from where there are superb views over the Vale of Aylesbury and of course of the Didcot power station cooling towers. The route descends into the Vale to Ellesborough village whose church is the parish church for Chequers. It climbs back onto the Chilterns through an archaeologically rich hillside and descends into the Chequers valley before climbing again through woodland back to the start.

MAP:
HARVEY Route Map Ridgeway; OS Landranger Sheet 165, OS Explorer No 181 Chiltern Hills North

START/FINISH:
Coombe Hill Car Park SP851062. The 323 bus goes through Ellesborough, so the walk could be adapted to start from Ellesborough church

DISTANCE:
5½ miles (9km)

APPROXIMATE TIME:
3 hours

HIGHEST POINT:
853ft (260m) Coombe Hill

REFRESHMENTS:
Ice Cream Van on Coombe Hill (occasionally)

ADVICE:
This is a morning or afternoon's walk without a pub or café en route, so take your own refreshments

A   Most of the Chequers estate was given to the nation by Lord Lee of Fareham but he gave the noted beauty spot of Coombe Hill to the National Trust in 1918. The Trust often have sheep grazing the downland grass and the area is still immensely popular, partly thanks to the car park about half a mile from the viewpoint. The hill and views of the hill from the Vale itself are dominated by the stone memorial column to the men of Buckinghamshire who died in the Boer War. It was built in 1904 and has a tall plinth with a tapering column or obelisk crowned by a ball and a golden flame, symbolising eternal life. Disaster struck in 1938 when, as a plaque states, it was almost totally destroyed by lightning and was rebuilt by the County Council, not surprisingly incorporating prominent lightning conductors this time.

The views from Coombe Hill at over 850ft (259m) are magnificent, looking out over the Vale of Aylesbury past Aylesbury itself to the Quainton hills, to the left of which you can see Waddesdon Manor, the great Rothschild French chateau on its tree-clad hill. Further left beyond the

Ellesborough Church and the Vale of Aylesbury from Coombe Hill

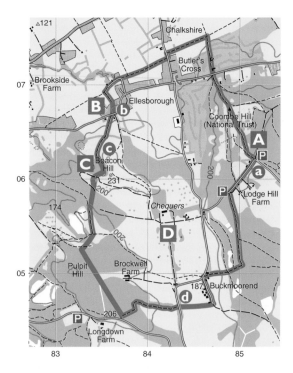

Chiltern escarpment are the ubiquitous Didcot Power Station cooling towers. In the immediate foreground below is the tower of Ellesborough church and further left is the bare grassy summit of Beacon Hill. You can even see Chequers house itself to the left of Beacon Hill.

a   Luckily, I managed to park in the shade at the Coombe Hill car park. Near the road end of the car park go through a gate

to take the central of three paths across downland to a wood, beyond which the Monument is at the end of a grassy ridge. Having admired the views and chatted to other walkers, I headed almost due north, down the centre of the ridge. Almost immediately the path drops steeply into woodland with dog roses and field roses twining in the bushes on its edge and along the path. The woodland is very varied: ash, mountain ash, oak, sycamore, hazel, beech and whitebeam, while there are meadow browns, graylings and speckled wood butterflies in profusion darting along the path or swirling in patches of summer sunlight.

Soon you will hear chatter from the Ellesborough golf course. Cross the road and go through a gate beside the Par 4 Number 1 Hole and follow the well-signed path through the golf course, with more speckled woods darting in the dappled sunshine. Soon leaving the golfers behind, climb a stile and continue straight on with a field on the right and sheep net fencing on the left. At a fence junction, turn left over another stile to follow the Aylesbury Ring waymarked path westward. Ahead is Ellesborough church with the grassy knoll of Beacon Hill to its left rearing out of the tree-clad slopes. When the path soon joins a track with views of Malt House Farm, a timber-framed farmhouse largely rebuilt in brick in 1672, across sheep

A green lane near Ellesborough

pasture. When the track reaches a road, turn briefly left, then right opposite Southfield Cottages, a row of altered brick and flint cottages. Now pass over a stile, still following the Aylesbury Ring through horse paddocks and across fields to a lane. A red admiral fluttered along beside me for many yards.

Follow the lane ahead past the Springs, a roughcast house dated 1911, then Springs Cottage, brick and flint and thatch; at the end of the lane cross two stiles with a spring source between and a spectacularly gnarled and stag-headed poplar beside them. Continue to the next stile and then turn left to go uphill to Ellesborough churchyard.

B The church of Saints Peter and Paul is mostly late 14th Century, but was heavily restored by the Victorians and completely refaced. Inside there is a good wall monument of 1638 to Bridget Croke of Chequers and a nice reredos by Comper of 1901. The church is beautifully situated with fine views from the churchyard but the views of its tall tower from far and wide along the Chilterns and from the Vale give it an importance well beyond its architectural qualities, together with the fact that numerous prime ministers, monarchs and presidents have been brought here from Chequers for Sunday worship over the years.

Outside the churchyard are a row of thatched cottages and opposite and almost out of sight are a set of homely almshouses, founded in 1746 by Lady Isabella Dodd, a Croke daughter from Chequers for the maintenance of four old men and four old women.

b From the churchyard, cross the main road to the bus stop and turn right alongside the Lady Dodd Almshouses picket fences, and left through a kissing gate into a grassy meadow to follow a diagonal path heading to the right of Beacon Hill, the high, bare downland spur protruding from the Chiltern escarpment and over 730ft (225m) above sea level.

c This stretch of the walk is rich in archaeological remains. In the woods about 200yds (180m) to the right of the path are earthworks known as Cymbeline's Castle. There is a tradition that the British king, Shakespeare's Cymbeline or Cunobelinus was buried here. Utter nonsense of course, for the earthworks are those of a Norman motte and bailey castle, although the name of the villages nearby, the Kimbles, may suggest a connection with the Iron Age leader. Also on Beacon Hill's slopes are a Bronze Age bowl barrow burial mound and a very well-preserved pillow mound. The latter is a medieval earthwork providing purpose-built rabbit breeding places. Rabbits were introduced into England in the 12th Century from France and were managed for their skins and the table. The mound is obviously associated with Ellesborough and Great

Thatched cottages near
Ellesborough Church

Kimble Warrens, which occupy two deep well-wooded combes immediately to the west.

Malt House Farm

c   Walk uphill on the path along the west flank of Beacon Hill, with the hill on your left. The path plunges into the cool of the woods along the edge of Ellesborough Warren with box trees and box scrub amid the more usual trees. The path climbs out of the Warren up wood-edged earth steps with virulent nettles, ground elder, wild garlic and herb robert in abundance. The path emerges onto pasture, then back into woodland, with coppiced sweet chestnut and sycamore and ash and beech trees above. Beyond the wood, continue south at gates with a finger post to cross the Ridgeway Path across a field. Continue in the same direction, diverging slightly from the fence on your left, uphill across pasture with parkland beeches, as well as invasive sycamore and ash scrub. Apart from buttercups and hawkweed there are many purple orchids on the slopes in summer while sheep laze in the shadow of the beeches.

Ignore a path along the open hillside to your left and head for the hill crest and trees, with a silver birch at the path's entrance into the woods and forget-me-nots aplenty. The usual Chiltern Society painted arrows on trees guide one through the wood. At a footpath junction bear left to follow bridleway arrows, this time with a blue centre painted in the arrow head. The path weaves amid the trees but keep following the bridleway blue-centred arrows for half a mile to turn left at a bridleway junction, continuing along the Icknield Way 'Rider's Route' signed on a post. There are occasional foxgloves in clearings and the path winds through woods with some very tall beeches, poplars, hornbeams and cherries. Soon you get views of Chequers House's south front, and the path enters a woodland strip of hornbeam, beech and ash and bluebells in spring, then continues to the road.

D Chequers House was rebuilt in 1565 for William Hawtrey whose family had owned the estate for over 300 years. It was a brick house with stone dressings and Hawtrey's north front remains virtually intact with large mullioned and transomed windows and five gables. The rest owes more to Reginald Blomfield in the 1890s for the then owner, Bertram Astley, and again in 1909–1910 for Arthur Lee, later Lord Lee of Fareham, who leased the house from 1909, finally succeeding in buying the estate in 1917. Having by then completed his restoration of the house and grounds Lord Lee and his wife, Ruth Moore an American heiress, donated the house and grounds to the nation as a retreat for prime ministers. They moved out in 1921 and since then all prime ministers, starting with Lloyd George and excepting only Bonar Law, have enjoyed the use of the house and grounds and innumerable foreign statesmen have visited and stayed as their guests.

d Cross the road, briefly following it left before the path turns right to cross a field. Pass to the right of a mid-1990s brick and flint farmhouse, Buckmoor End Farmhouse. At the lane, turn left to walk past the farmhouse and farmbuildings on the left and a range of estate cottages bearing a plaque 'L of F 1920', indicating they were built for Lord Lee of Fareham. At the road turn right onto the Ridgeway Path, which has just emerged from the security-camera observed Chequers parkland opposite. Follow it up through Goodmerhill Wood east, then at the top of the hill turn left, continuing on the Ridgeway to the Chequers to Coombe Hill road, near Lodge Hill Game Farm, and at the road turn right to return to the car park.

A view accross the vale of Aylesbury

THE HAMPDENS

This 7-mile walk has as its highlight Hampden House in its parkland, the seat of John Hampden 'the Patriot' who defied King Charles I over the Ship Money tax. The walk also includes one of the best stretches of the Iron Age linear earthwork Grim's Dyke in the Chilterns and the delightful church of Little Hampden with its timber-framed porch-cum-belfry.

A This walk starts in the Whiteleaf Hill Car Park, as did Walk 22, but leaves it in the opposite direction. After a mile or so the route reaches the linear earthwork named Grim's Ditch, a name of great antiquity used to describe mysterious earthworks believed by the credulous to be the work of giants or Gods, Grim being another name for Odin. Be that as it may, the name is applied to a number of linear earthworks, not only in

MAP:
HARVEY Route Map
Ridgeway; OS Landranger
Sheet 165, OS Explorer No
181 Chiltern Hills North

START/FINISH:
Whiteleaf Hill Car Park
SP823035. There are no bus
routes to this car park, but
the 323 and 324 buses stop
in Monks Risborough and
you could walk uphill to the
car park, adding 1 mile
(1.6 km) to the walk

DISTANCE:
6½ miles (10km)

APPROXIMATE TIME:
3 hours

HIGHEST POINT:
810ft (247m) Kop Hill, near
start of walk

REFRESHMENTS:
The Rising Sun PH, Little
Hampden Common
SP857040

ADVICE:
This walk is mainly on the
Chilterns plateau and is
undulating rather than steep
with the only steepish
descent and ascent across
a valley

Hampden House, the west front

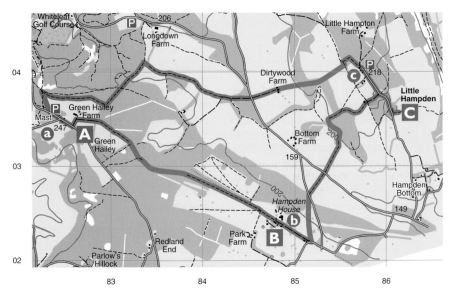

Buckinghamshire, but elsewhere as in Middlesex or Oxfordshire and reappears in walks 25 and 30. At one time thought to be an Anglo-Saxon estate boundary, most archaeologists now think it to be from the Iron Age and dug as a communal boundary dividing up hill pastures and commons, presumably between the communities in the valley to the north and those on the plateau to the south. The Ditch ran from Naphill Common to Lacey Green (Walk 21) to turn sharply towards Hampden House which it passes before disappearing to reappear in Walk 25. What is clear is that it is not a military boundary and was dug when the Chilterns were open pasture. The stretch the route follows is one of the best, with a high bank to the north and a lower bank on the south side of the ditch.

a   Leaving Whiteleaf Hill Car Park by the vehicle entrance turn left and walk past Green Hailey Water Tower, passing the turning to Kop Hill on the right (sign-posted to Princes Risborough), a very steep hill that was used for hill climb motor trials until the 1920s. Soon, turn left at a public bridleway sign onto the drive to Green Hailey Farm, then right just before the farm through a galvanised six bar gate onto a surfaced lane. On the left was a field of linseed with a view to Aylesbury beyond. Past some satellite dishes cross a footpath junction onto a path alongside woods on the left with honeysuckle in flower climbing some of the trees and occasional foxgloves. The path then descends with a blackthorn and hawthorn hedge on the right and yellow meadow vetchling and white rough chervil. Enter the woods past a broken gate and continue straight on, following white painted arrows on the trees, ignoring all paths to left and right, noting hazel coppice and clearings bright with foxgloves amid the beech trees. The path crosses a valley within the woods and soon passes through Grim's Ditch which can be seen on both sides of the path as a deep ditch with banks on either side. Continuing straight on, Grim's Ditch gradually comes closer to the path, having made its right-angle turn. Here the north bank is still over six feet high, and both the bank and the ditch and lower, south bank are planted with beech trees and are well grassed. The path is parallel to the Ditch for half a mile (0.8km), with a hedge in-between festooned with rock and dog roses in flower and on the right occasional parkland trees amid the crops, mostly limes with a few oaks. The Ditch eventually merges with the path as you approach Hampden House, which becomes visible with a magnificent cedar twice its height to its left. Pass through a gate onto the drive.

B   Hampden House is a remarkable building which in recent times enjoyed fame as the home of Hammer House of Horror films. Now it is well cared for by an insurance company. The exterior is mostly 18th-Century in appearance and the older house was remodelled in Strawberry Hill Gothic style. This predates Walpole's Strawberry Hill by a few years, to which it owes the battlements and the ogee-arched windows and the deep recessed porch that we see as we approach along the footpath. However, the house has a core much older than the 1740 to 1757 work. There is a late 15th-Century battlemented tower known as King John's Tower and a late 16th-Century great hall and west block of about 1680.

St Mary's Church, Great Hampden

All this work brackets the dates of the most famous member of the Hampden family: John (1594–1643). This John, 'the Patriot' and an MP for Buckinghamshire, refused to pay Charles I's Ship Money tax in 1637 and was arrested in a room in the house. When Civil War broke out he was prominent among its leaders and was mortally wounded at Chalgrove Field fighting for Parliament and died in a house in Thame, Oxfordshire, in June 1643.

Opposite the house are the former stables, now offices, which were also Gothicised in the 1740s, and nearby the parish church of St Mary. Inside is a fine monument to John Hampden which includes a relief of him receiving his fatal wound. This was erected in 1743, his death centenary, but unfortunately the church is usually locked.

b Continuing along the drive past the church, parkland is on both sides. Diagonally to the right, immediately past the church, a lime avenue has lost most of its ancient limes. The drive itself passes through an avenue of horse chestnuts, limes and planes. At a pair of semi-detached Lodges of about 1900 in flint and brick with elaborate gable timberwork, go through an electrically opened six bar gate, and then immediately left over a stile into a meadow. This path gives views of the more formal east front of Hampden house with battlemented two-storey side wings and a three storey central block which looks east down The Glade, a grassed strip over a mile long cut through woodland and terminated by the Pepper Boxes, a pair of 1744 lodges. The path crosses one stile and continues to descend a second. Cross the road and follow a hedge between oat fields. It is a good hedge with several species: hazel, hawthorn, holly, elder, blackthorn or sloe, dogwood and hedge maple, (also dogrose and honeysuckle in summer) and thus, possibly 600 years old. Cross the main road and continue alongside another good ancient hedge, this time on the right hand side, climbing out of the valley and into Warren Wood.

The path winds and climbs through beech and hazel coppice as well as oaks, ashes, thorn and wood maple, together with wild flowers such as herb robert. At a footpath junction turn right, staying within the edge of the woodland with arable land beyond. The wood gradually narrows until it becomes a green lane into Little Hampden, passing the mid-18th-Century, brick-fronted and box-sash windowed, Little Hampden Farm on the right. At the junction, turn right to walk downhill to visit Little Hampden church. Return back up the road and keep going until you reach the pub.

C Little Hampden is little more than a straggle of cottages and houses with the church at the south end. This dates mainly from the 13th Century, with contemporary wall paintings but curiously its dedication is unknown. Its most attractive feature externally is the 15th-Century timber-framed north porch, with a belfry upper storey containing a single bell. On the opposite side of the lane is Manor Farm, a cruck-framed 15th-Century hall with a 17th-Century crosswing, and a farmyard with two mid-18th-Century weatherboarded and tile-roofed barns. At the north end of the village is the Rising Sun pub offering welcome refreshment.

c Leave the Rising Sun and continue along the track, then turn left past a cottage, not carrying on to the drive to Hampden Manor. At a 'No Horse Riding on the Common' sign turn left and, the bridleway soon forking to the right, take the left-hand footpath to pass through a holly, ash and horse chestnut coppice. On emerging from the coppice, cross a track and walk alongside hedges and then down beside a wood before entering it where you follow yellow arrows painted on trees descending through the wood and, at a fork in the path marked by a double headed arrow, bear left and descend. At the edge of the wood, carry straight on (yellow arrow) with views of Chequers away to the right and, skirting Dirtywood Farm; continue on to the main road in the valley bottom.

A plane tree in the avenue on the drive to Hampden House

Cross the road onto the 'Private Road to Solinger House' and follow this through woods, then wood on the left only and a hedge on the right with vetch and hedge woundwort in the verge. Where the road swings left carry straight on through a gap in the hedge to walk along the right-hand side of a hedge heading westward with cuckoo spit on much of the dogwood in the hedge. Carry on past Cross Coppice with meadow beside the path, with much vetch and trefoil and of course lots of golden buttercups in the summer. Continue with a double hedge on your left and where the wood angles to the right go into it over two stiles to descended to the valley bottom and turn left at a footpath junction onto a bridleway marked by white arrows with a blue centre. The bridleway climbs gently, if horse-churned muddily, with a field on the left beyond the

The timber-framed porch at
Little Hampden Church

wood-edge hedge of hazel. Ignoring a footpath crossroads, keep on the bridleway that is now fully in the woods and ignoring a footpath signed to the right, climb steadily with herb robert, foxgloves, buttercups and melilot in the sunnier summer patches.

At the summit by a post, turn right onto another bridleway, with fields on the left, keeping within the edge of the beech woods with occasional glimpses over the Vale of Aylesbury and to the bluff of Pulpit Hill to the right. Keep on the bridleway until emerging onto a path junction, which you cross to reach the Ridgeway Path. Go left onto the Path and soon left again back to the car park.

THE LEE

This walk starts and finishes in The Lee, the village transformed by the founder of Liberty's store in Regent Street, Arthur Lasenby Liberty. He created the village green and enlarged the parish church. The walk route heads north-west to the Ridgeway Path, via the hamlet of King's Ash, and follows the Path climbing in woodland up the Chiltern escarpment to Cock's Hill, where it crosses Grim's Ditch and heads back to The Lee via Swan Bottom.

MAP:
HARVEY Route Map Ridgeway; OS Landranger Sheet 165, OS Explorer No 181 Chiltern Hills North

START/FINISH:
The Lee Village Green SP900042. The No 59 bus travels from Great Missenden to Chesham and stops in The Lee, but it is not a frequent service

DISTANCE:
5½ miles (9km)

APPROXIMATE TIME:
2½ hours

HIGHEST POINT:
About 770ft (235m) at Grim's Ditch SP895067

REFRESHMENTS:
The Cock and Rabbit in The Lee, Old Swan at Swan Bottom, both depending upon the time of day

ADVICE:
Much is on the Chiltern plateau and the only major decent/ascent is down to the Ridgeway Path and back up to the plateau

A   The Lee is a parish that appears to have been carved out of Wendover parish in the Middle Ages and certainly by the 13th Century, judging by the date of parts of its parish church. Some of its parish boundaries are of great antiquity, in particular the northern one which follows the curiously named Arrewig Lane, which is probably over 1,500 years old. It started as a double boundary bank between early Anglo-Saxon estates, the centre of which became a lane.

The Lee village owes its present character to Arthur Lasenby Liberty, the son of a Chesham draper and lace manufacturer

who went on to great things and founded Liberty's store in Regent Street. The store, in its present form, was built in the1920s for his son and is partly stone-faced and partly timber-framed, using timbers from the last two wooden-walled Royal Navy warships, the 'Admiral Lord Howe' and the 'Hindustan', built in 1860. The figurehead from the 'Admiral Lord Howe' was brought to The Lee and peers over a hedge south of the village near the Stewart-Liberty's house, Pipers, to frighten passing motorists.

The War Memorial, The Lee village green

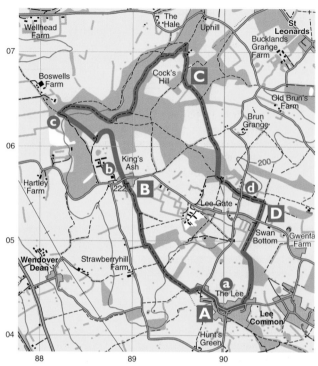

Liberty, who had bought the Manor House in 1901, created a village green by the simple expedience of pulling down all the cottages on the south side of the lane. In their place, he built a pub, The Cock and Rabbit of 1907, and a pair of cottages in 1908, Patchwicks and Rushmere, both designed in the Arts and Crafts style. He also had the Victorian parish church extended and his grave has an Art Nouveau-influenced Celtic cross by Archibald Knox. The hand of the Liberty family has created a delightful village with older buildings surviving on the north side of the green.

a Parking near the Cock and Rabbit pub, there is much to admire around the green, including a World War I memorial in the style of the Celtic cross, probably also by Archibald Knox. Walk across the green away from the pub and briefly along the road before turning into the churchyard. It is worth lingering inside, for on the right is the Celtic cross memorial to Arthur Lasenby Liberty who died in 1917 and his wife Dame Emma Louise. The Victorian church of the 1860s in brick with stone dressings was enlarged, altered and its interior fitted out in Liberty style in 1910. It has a foundation stone on the north chancel wall inscribed 'relaid by Emma Louise Liberty on

Enlargement of Church 14th October 1910'. The churchyard is a nature conservation area and wild flowers grow here in profusion and it attracts butterflies such as red admirals, ringlets, grayling and the ubiquitous meadow brown.

Follow the path to the old parish church, built of flint with chalkstone or clunch dressings. It is mainly 13th-Century with an 18th-Century brick porch and inside there are some 14th-Century wall paintings. It is serene and beautiful little church. Leaving the churchyard near the nave over a stile by Church Farm, a 17th-Century timber-framed house cased in brick and enlarged in the 18th Century, cross to another stile by a wall to follow. The Chiltern Link waymarked path leads diagonally away from the farmhouse across a meadow with 18th Century and later farmbuildings to the right. Over a stile by a gate, leave the earthwork enclosure that surrounds both churches and Church Farm. Ignoring the footpath to the left, continue almost straight on, going to the right of a hazel hedge which you follow with arable land to the right.

At the Sign of the Cock and Rabbit, The lee

This is a most pleasant stretch of walking on grassy tracks alongside fine hedges and follows the Chiltern Link waymarked route all the way to the Ridgeway Path junction. The hedge has thorn, maple, hazel, elder, holly and ash with small oak standards. Past an ash and oak wood with the welcoming sign 'Warning Traps Set in This Wood', the path goes to the left of the hedge which also has dogwood and blackthorn in it which, on a species count, makes it at least 600 years old. After three fields you reach a hedge where the path curves left and after about 50 yards (46m) go right over a stile to follow a hedge between fields, then over a stile by a gate, across a meadow to a stile on the other side of the field which leads onto a path. Straight opposite there is a small gate leading onto the drive to Kings Ash Barn to the road.

B Kings Ash is barely a hamlet, centred upon Kings Ash Farm which has a farmhouse of about 1700, altered in the 19th Century, with chequer brick elevations. You can see the bricked -up openings of several of the 18th-Century window openings. Its weatherboarded and slate roofed barns have been well converted to houses, The East Barn and Kings Ash Barn. Opposite are a pair of Liberty farm cottages, again in a sort of Arts and Crafts style, as in The Lee itself.

b Across the road, still following the Chiltern Link path, climb a stile into a meadow with foxgloves and betony in the summer months and over another stile into lush meadow. Follow the left

The path north-west of The Lee

hand hedge accompanied by meadow brown and gate keeper butterflies and then along the left edge of Barn Wood: beech, oak, ash, horse chestnut and sycamore trees and a boundary hedge of hazel, blackthorn, thorn and holly, all festooned with dog roses in summer. The path curves round towards a farm called 'Concord' with rendered elevations, many gables and a slate roof. Right over a stile and there is a white painted signpost pointing to Wendover in one direction and The Lee in the other with 'Concord 750 feet' painted on the post. Walk between the farm and its outbuildings, cross another stile into pasture to follow the path which soon enters a wood where the path descends and after about 400 yards (366m) continues beside a sunken lane, Hogtrough Lane, to the Ridgeway Path junction.

C After leaving the Ridgeway Path the route crosses Grim's Ditch, another section of the long Iron Age linear earthwork that runs from north of High Wycombe to Great Hampden (Walk 24), then intermittently across the Wendover-Missenden valley, reappearing strongly in The Lee parish to head across the Tring Salient of Hertfordshire to the Pitstone Hills (Walk 30). This route crosses it at a good and prominent section of this great boundary marker.

c Turn right at the Ridgeway Path junction, still within Barn Wood, and follow it initially along the valley bottom with some conifers amid the ash, beech, oak and sycamore. At a fork the Path bears right to climb gradually through hazel coppice with a stand of pines on the right, then climbing more steeply with occasional tall silver birch. Continue to follow the Ridgeway path signs and the yellow acorn markers. The Path eventually levels out with foxgloves in clearings and becomes wider with margins of bracken and bramble. The wild flower species now increase with more daylight reaching the path: in summer, woundwort, tall great mullein or Aaron's rod, St John's wort, herb robert and others can be seen in profusion.

Ignoring two footpaths to the left, turn right at a footpath crossroads and, past masses of foxgloves, head for a gate. The path passes houses and yards at Cock's Hill to emerge over an unusual brick step through stile into pasture. Follow the right hand side of a tall hedge mostly of thorn and holly, then through a gap in the woods ahead. Within the wood belt is Grim's Ditch to left and right, the ditch deep on the left hand side and the bank high on the right.

From the wood, cross a field, through another wood belt with a staggered fence stile. This is the ancient parish boundary between The Lee and Wendover. Emerging, walk across two large fields with long views south, heading for a wood, Lordling Wood, where buzzards are often seen hovering. Follow the path through the beech wood interspersed with tall oaks and with the occasional smell of stinkhorn, with white arrows painted on some trees. Out of the wood continue on a track between houses and garages, honeysuckle in the hedges and rosebay willow herb in the verges, now joining the Chiltern Way waymarked path, reaching the road at The Old Swan pub.

King's Ash Farmhouse

d Cross the road and climb a stile to the right of the drive to Kingswood House to walk along grass between a hedge on the left and post-and-wire paddocks on the right. Passing the front of Kingswood House, built about 1900, the path passes between sycamore and ashes. A noisy pheasant blundered into the air as I approached. Over a stile turn right and follow the path to cross the road at Swan Bottom and onto the drive to Kingvale Farm, then through a succession of paddocks with a thick hedge to your left to reach a wood belt where I disturbed a yaffle or green woodpecker. Turning left into the wood walk along the muddy central path to a footpath junction marked by a two headed arrow where you turn right. Leave the wood over a stile into cattle pasture to walk uphill to the road beside a converted barn, Home Farm Barn, and at the road turn right to walk past Swyllmer, a Liberty altered house, back to the village green of The Lee.

WENDOVER AND HALTON

MAP:
HARVEY Route Map
Ridgeway; OS Landranger
Sheet 165, OS Explorer No
181 Chiltern Hills North

START/FINISH:
Wendover, High Street Car
Park SP868077. Wendover
Station is on the Chiltern
Line from Marylebone to
Aylesbury and is in Pound
Street, actually on the
Ridgeway Path route. The
town is also on several bus
routes

DISTANCE/ASCENT:
6½ miles (10.5km), 426ft
(130m)

APPROXIMATE TIME:
2½ hours

HIGHEST POINT:
807ft (246m) on Boddington
Hill SP884082

REFRESHMENTS:
A good range in Wendover
from pubs to cafes and
restaurants

ADVICE:
This starts as a two-mile
walk along a canal towpath,
which is easy level walking.
The route also passes
through the RAF camp at
Halton so take care to keep
to the public path. The climb
into Wendover Woods is long
and gradual, rather than
short and sharp

Wendover is one of few towns on the Ridgeway Path and is a most attractive market town. The route follows a stretch of the Wendover Arm of the Grand Union Canal opened in 1797 and then skirts the grounds of Halton House, one of the Buckinghamshire country houses of a member of the Rothschild banking family, now an RAF station. It then climbs into Wendover Woods and passes within 600 yards (549m) of the highest point in the Chiltern Hills at 876ft (267m).

A Wendover developed around the church and this area still has a distinctly village feel, for after it became a borough with a market in the 13th Century, a new town was laid out further north along the present High Street and Aylesbury Road. Further growth before 1700 took place along Tring Road, including Coldharbour Cottages, a long range of thatched cottages, Pound Street and South Street. The best of these is Aylesbury Road with good Georgian fronts to timber-framed houses and some timber-frames, including the jettied No 9.

a From the car park off High Street turn right to walk towards the clocktower at its junction with Tring Road and Aylesbury Road. This started off as an 1842 market hall (a very small one) but had the clock tower added in 1870, the lower part being adapted as a fire appliance store. Now it is an information centre. Turn left into Aylesbury Road and then right into Wharf Road: an evocative name and indeed after 200 yards (183m) turn left onto the towpath of the Wendover Arm of the Grand Union Canal at a footpath sign.

Cottages in Pound Street,
Wendover

B The Wendover Arm was built by the Grand Junction Canal Company and opened in 1797. It is 6 miles (9.6km) long and had a twin purpose: to providing access for trade and to supply water to top up the Marsworth Flight of locks as canals are not self-renewing rivers and each use of a lock reduces the water 'uphill' of it. The problem was that the canal leaked badly and sometimes even drew water from the main Grand Junction Canal: an outcome not exactly intended. This walk follows part of the section still with water in it, for between Drayton Beauchamp and Little Tring the canal was drained after a stop lock was installed at Little Tring in 1904 and much of this dry stretch is followed in Walk 28.

b This section was restored in 1993 and is a pretty walk with reed margins to the canal, often overhung by trees. Wild flowers in summer include lesser burdock, rose bay and great willowherb. After about a mile the canal widens to a reed and cress bed with some willows and aspens as well as ash, beech and poplar behind. This is the area known as The Wides, with willowherb and reedmace growing in the drying reed beds. Beyond this area, the canal passes under an ornate road bridge, its cast iron balustrades with a palmette frieze. A greater range of wild flowers soon appear, including meadowsweet, cresses, bittersweet, horsetails and cuckoo pint.

A bridge on the Wendover Arm of the Grand Union Canal

Past the barns now converted to houses at Lower Farm, I left the canal at a modern bridge and turned right into Halton village. Carry on as far as the public footpath sign by the double gates leading into the churchyard. Go through the gates and follow the path round in front of the church.

C Halton village has a number of houses built or modified by the Rothschilds who had bought the estate in 1853. Most of the changes date from Baron Alfred Charles' time and some cottages had a frieze added showing the trade of the occupant. The parish church of St Michael and All Angels was built in 1813 for the Dashwoods whose principal seat was at West Wycombe. It is built in Denner Hill stone, a hard stone found in the Chilterns above High Wycombe as used by Wyatt at Windsor Castle and at Wycombe Abbey in the late 18th and early 19th Centuries. In the churchyard are 200

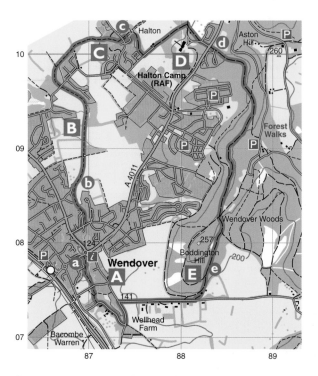

Commonwealth War Graves Commission headstones, for airmen and soldiers who have died at Halton, the RAF camp nearby. The earliest is 1915 and, at present, the latest is 1995. One includes the verse 'Oh for the touch of a vanished hand, And the sound of a voice that is stilled'. The World War II headstones include 12 Polish pilots and one Dutchman, some military nurses and a few soldiers – a most moving visit.

c   Leave the churchyard through a kissing gate beyond the church and then turned immediately left on grass to head into some horse chestnuts, limes and sycamores. Follow the guide posts and turn right onto a metalled track, running through an avenue of limes, yews, horse chestnuts and sycamores, with rugby fields beyond on the left. At a junction with a tarmacked road turn left, now well within Halton Camp. As this right of way passes through a military site, keep carefully to the official route, following the road uphill with sports fields on the left and woods on the right with yew and juniper amid the trees, some deciduous and some coniferous. At a sharp bend, leave the road and go over a stile on the left-hand side and onto a metalled path going uphill through woods with yews on either side. The road you have just left curves through the wood to Halton House and back again to where the path rejoins. At the road turn left to reach Upper Icknield Way, here the A4011 and, in crossing straight over, leave the Halton House grounds and the RAF camp.

D Halton House was built for Baron Alfred de Rothschild in the 1880s and was in the style of a French chateau with tall pavilion roofs. Alfred had his own private circus and was a familiar sight around the area in his trap pulled by zebra. He died in 1918 and the estate was bought by the RAF, his house becoming the officers' mess.

d Across the A4011, walk straight on through a gate onto a track through the woods and into Wendover Woodland Park (as indicated on the sign). Ignoring a footpath off to the right continue up the metalled track, steadily climbing and ignoring paths to right and left. The woodland is mostly beech with yews, lime, juniper and a good range of wild flowers in summer, such as clematis, rosebay willowherb in clearings, lesser burdock, marjoram, wild basil, agrimony, betony and St John's wort. Horse chestnuts and ashes also begin to appear.

St Michael and All Angels Church, Halton

Stay on the metalled track and at a Y-junction, where the bridleway ends, take the right fork where the woods become exclusively beech. Ignore turnings to left and right, noting banks of woundwort and pass a clearing with a flint walled enclosure cut into the hill slope and a semi-circle of yew hedges on the path edge focused on a stone pillar erected in memory of John Sale, Forestry Commision District Officer. The little plateau here was obviously constructed as a good viewpoint, probably for Baron Alfred, and gives long views to Coombe Hill and over the Vale of Aylesbury.

Further on a track merges from the right and clustered bellflowers appear in the verges. Beyond a picnic site in a clearing there is the start of a Fitness Trail, a route with various exercise bars at intervals for the visitor who needs a more structured open air leisure. At the vehicle turning circle

RAF Graves in Halton
Churchyard

turn left onto a bridleway, which soon becomes a metalled track. Over the crest start to descend and, at a Y-junction, bear right at horseshoe post no 5, onto a track running parallel to the ridge, before descending steeply along the flanks of Boddington Hill. This section can be muddy in places.

E Boddington Hill is an Iron Age hill fort built at the end of a spur dominating the way through the Chilterns from Wendover south-east along the Misbourne valley. The ditch and bank surround about 17 acres and Iron Age pottery has been found. Its highest point is 843ft (257m), but its impact from far away is nowhere near that of those along the Berkshire Downs in earlier walks as it lies within woodland, like Pulpit Hill near Whiteleaf (Walks 22 and 23).

e The track descends steeply and then levels out where houses become visible on the left beyond the trees. At a fork, go left to descend to the road at a one bar gate, turning right to walk along the road, Hale Lane, which has wide verges and modern houses on the left, usually with the name 'Boddington' incorporated in their names. There are good views looking back to Boddington Hill itself. At the T-junction (with modern houses opposite) turn left and walk along the pavement on the far side. At a letter box on a post pick up the Ridgeway Path emerging from a lane on the left and turn right (signposted St Mary's Church) to walk down Church Lane, passing Wendover House School on the left.

Its stable block by the road is dated 1735 and the house, formerly the manor house was rebuilt in the 1870s by George Devey, an architect much used by the Rothschilds as well. Beyond, I visited the parish church, much restored by Victorian architects, before rejoining the Ridgeway Path which goes down Heron Path with a pretty pond on the left. For a while it follows the banks of a stream, then passes in front of an elegant stucco house with a 19th-Century front, Bucksbridge House, before becoming a path between gardens and on the right the former National School of 1868, which is now a collection of houses. Emerging at the east end of the High Street I turned left to walk back to the car park, having explored other streets in the town. My visit took me to Back Lane – including Vine House, draped in vines, a timber-framed house with an 18th-Century refronting – and the ranges of cottages in Pound Street.

CHOLESBURY AND ST LEONARDS

This walk, a relatively gentle one, starts on one of the chalk ridges, separated by dry valleys that converge on the market town of Chesham. The route starts in one of the strung out settlements along this ridge, Cholesbury, which has a good Iron Age hill fort, heads north-west into Hertfordshire, then follows the Ridgeway Path, before heading back to Cholesbury via Grim's Ditch and the hamlet of St Leonards.

A Cholesbury was a very small parish encompassing little more than the Common and the hill fort, gaining St Leonards and Buckland Common from Aston Clinton and Drayton Beauchamp respectively. These had been very long and narrow parishes with their villages in the vale below amid rich arable land, their commons, heaths and woodland up in the Chilterns, the parish boundaries being of great antiquity.

Cholesbury's St Laurence church, rebuilt apart from the nave south wall in 1873, stands in one corner of an Iron Age hill fort whose double bank and ditch enclose about 10 acres. In parts the fort is protected by three banks and two ditches and the ditches are deep and wide, in places over 50ft (15.3m) across and 12ft (3.7m) deep. The church has a good 13th-Century south doorway within its Victorian porch and a charming louvred bellcote at the west end of the nave, also Victorian.

a From the Common, walk west towards the Village Hall, built in 1895, and climb a stile to its left, go along an access track, now within Cholesbury Camp, and over another stile into a pasture field. Ignoring a footpath to the right climb another stile and turn left to visit the church which is usually locked, although the keyholders are listed in the porch. Return to the footpath route heading for a gate beneath beech trees with a stile beside it. Over the stile pause to admire the deep ditch and high banks of the Iron Age hill fort which stretch away on each side within a belt of beech trees.

Continue along a grassy track, its verges rich in melilot and buttercups in summer, then through scrubby woodland with hazel to the left. After another stile and some better trees, mainly oak and beech, leave the wood over a stile to cross a paddock, with an overgrown hedge of thorn and hazel with some taller oak standards on left. At the next stile, enter a

MAP:
HARVEY Route Map Ridgeway; OS Landranger Sheet 165, OS Explorer No 181 Chiltern Hills North

START/FINISH:
Cholesbury Common SP932071. The No 94 bus from Tring to Chesham stops in Cholesbury, otherwise there is no public transport access to the start of this walk

DISTANCE:
6 miles (9.5km)

APPROXIMATE TIME:
2½ hours

HIGHEST POINT:
800ft (244m) at Pavis Wood on the Ridgeway Path SP914092

REFRESHMENTS:
There are no shops or pubs on the route, but there are three pubs in Buckland Common and one further east along Cholesbury Common, near the former windmill

ADVICE:
This is a short walk but if hot take water or a drink as there are no pubs or shops along the route. The terrain is easy going

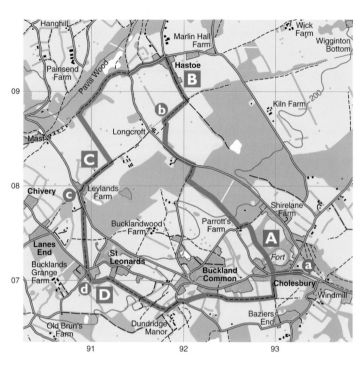

St Laurence's Church,
Cholesbury

much larger wood, mainly beech, but with silver birch and holly. Immediately turn left along the inner edge of the wood. Ignore a stile on the left and continue forward, soon bearing right to move away from the edge of the wood to walk parallel to it about 30 yards (27.4m) or so inside the wood. (A much-used, but undesignated path, follows more closely to the edge, and in muddy conditions, after wet weather, this would be a better option.) The two paths merge when the designated path moves back close to the edge before eventually reaching a stile at the angle of the wood. Over the stile, turn right onto a muddy track between post and wire fences leading to a road.

Here you turn left along Shire Lane, the boundary between Hertfordshire, on the right, and Buckinghamshire on the left. This is an ancient boundary, probably over a 1000 years old and may be a double boundary bank in which the space between has become a lane. Pass on the left Draytonwood House, a large house with a tile hung upper floor and timber-framed gables of about 1890. At a small beechwood on the right, climb a stile waymarked 'Chiltern Way', to walk through a hazel and holly undergrowth in what had been a hazel coppice with beech standards. Leaving the wood, head diagonally left across an arable field, Longcroft Farm, a late 19th-Century complex to the left. On reaching a narrow wood, turn right, still on the Chiltern Way, to follow Grim's Ditch within the belt of trees.

B   Grim's Ditch here is part of a boundary bank and ditch that runs from King's Ash (Walk 25) to Wigginton, a distance of nearly four miles. This is part of that great Iron Age earthwork feature that crops up in many of the walks in this book and this stretch is a good one with the bank in places 8ft (2.44m) above the ditch, which is to its right or south.

b   Walk along beside Grim's Ditch, which almost disappears as a ground feature just before you reach a bridleway that crosses the Ditch. Turn left to walk along a good green lane where scabious, trefoils, vetch, nipplewort, rosebay willowherb and feverfew can be seen in summer on the verges between the hawthorn hedges. Beyond some former farm labourers estate cottages the lane descends to Hastoe Farm, its 19th Century brick barns converted to houses.

Cholesbury Camp hillfort, the ditch and rampart

At the road junction, join the Ridgeway Path, turning left onto Gadmore Lane which goes steadily uphill. Where the lane turns left, the Ridgeway Path, and also the Ickenield Way Riding Trail, carry straight on through a gate into Pavis Wood. It is a broad metalled track in beech woods with glimpses of long views north off the ridge to the right. Amid the beech is some hornbeam, ash, oak, hazel and holly as well as firs. Where another path crosses, turn left to leave the Ridgeway Path, roughly on the Drayton Beauchamp/Buckland parish boundary, emerging into a large arable field. The path crosses the field well away from the hedge that marked the parish boundary to the left. This is not straight but follows the classic aratral curve, the elongated S plan produced by the medieval ox or horse plough team preparing to turn well ahead of the end of the strip they were ploughing. These S-curve hedges are always a sign of medieval ploughing and fossilise an ancient landscape. At the end of the field climb a stile and turn right into a lane.

C   The lane follows the course of Grim's Ditch with the ditch bank on the right and presumably the ditch itself the lane. The hedge has bittersweet with a purple flower and much wild basil

Footpath signage clutter

in summer. The earlier stretch of Grim's Ditch on this walk is more impressive.

c Pass through Leylands Farm to the road and turn left with a beechwood to your left within which are a pair of 1880s former estate cottages in vernacular style with timber-framed upper floors and sweeping eaves. At the drive on the right to boarding kennels, climb a stile to cross a pasture diagonally, then two arable fields to emerge over a stile with brick piers onto a road. On the right is the Victorian former National School, built in 1862 but now a house. Cross the road to St Leonards church.

D St Leonards church was built in the late 14th Century as a chapel of ease built for the upland parishioners of Aston Clinton whose parish church lies some four miles away in the vale beyond the Chilterns. By the 17th Century it was a ruin, but it was then restored and received its present roof. In the 1840s it assumed its present form and is an attractive small church, its walls rendered and colourwashed and the nave with a small tiled pyramid spire to its bell turret.

d Leave the churchyard by the gate with a lantern above it and turn left onto what may be an overgrown path in summer months. At the corner of the churchyard, go over a stile to follow a path diagonally left through pasture fields, a playing field, arable fields, a concrete drive and two more fields. Reaching a gate turn left onto the drive of Dundridge Manor, a moated 16th-Century farmhouse complete with a modern drawbridge and portcullis. The moat is a deep one, part with water and part dry. The drive passes along an avenue of beech trees and the right of way leaves through the left-hand pair of brick gate piers onto Oak Lane. Turn right onto the road and after about 40 yards (36m), opposite a house, go over a stile on the left into a paddock, heading diagonally right to a double stile in a row of lime trees. After this, the path heads diagonally left through fenced paddocks to a stile in the bottom left-hand corner at the rear of houses and an enclosed path, the boundary hedge of houses on the left and wire fence on the right. At the next stile (crosspaths), with a row of conifers extending to the right, continue ahead along the dry valley, with the hedge on the left, through two arable fields. Go forward into a pasture field and at the next crosspaths, turn left to go uphill in a field with a fence on the right, following the line of the overhead power cables. Leave the field over a stile, where a path between gardens leads to the road and Cholesbury. Turn right to walk past the village hall to your starting point.

TRING AND THE GRAND UNION CANAL

The late 18th Century Grand Union Canal, formerly the Grand Junction Canal, winds through the Chilterns and this walk follows its deep cutting to Bulbourne and the Tring Summit, its highest point, where it starts its descent into the Vale of Aylesbury by means of the Marsworth Flight of locks. The route also skirts three of the four large reservoirs dug by the canal company in the 1830s to supplement the water pumped from the Wendover Arm, a branch canal of 1797 that leaked badly and whose disused course the route also follows.

A Tring was the main medieval market town in the salient of Hertfordshire that projects into Buckinghamshire from the Tring Gap which had long provided a major route through the Chilterns, including the Roman road known as Akeman Street, now the A41. Architecturally the town is a little disappointing, but the medieval parish church is good and within has a spectacular Baroque monument of 1707 with Lord and Lady Gore reclining on the plinth of a huge urn. The High Street has a few good buildings, including the Bell pub, a former coaching inn, while the Rose and Crown Hotel opposite the church is a Rothschild period timber-framed Elizabethan style small country house.

a Park in the free car park near the church and, after visiting the church, turn right into the High Street. Between the Nat West and HSBC banks is an alley, a public footpath. Follow this south out of town, turning left for a short distance at an early T-junction and over the A41 by-pass.

B Tring Park house was bought in 1872 by Lionel Rothschild, a scion of the great banking family

Saints Peter and Paul Parish Church, Tring

MAP:
HARVEY Route Map Ridgeway; OS Landranger Sheet 165, OS Explorer No 181 Chiltern Hills North

START/FINISH:
Tring, Car Park to west of parish church SP923115, accessed from Frogmore St. Tring Station on the Euston line is about 2 miles east of the town centre.
Alternatively the walk could start from the station. Tring is on a few bus routes, including the 500 and 501 from Watford to Aylesbury

DISTANCE:
9½ miles (16km)

APPROXIMATE TIME:
4 hours

HIGHEST POINT:
721ft (220m) at Wigginton SP934105

REFRESHMENTS:
There is a choice in Tring, including The Bell pub. Out on the walk there are the Grand Junction Arms at Bulbourne, and the Bluebell Tea Rooms and the White Lion pub at Startops End

ADVICE:
About 4 miles of the walk is on canal towpaths which are level walking. The only real climb is up the Chiltern escarpment in Tring Park and the descent from Wigginton

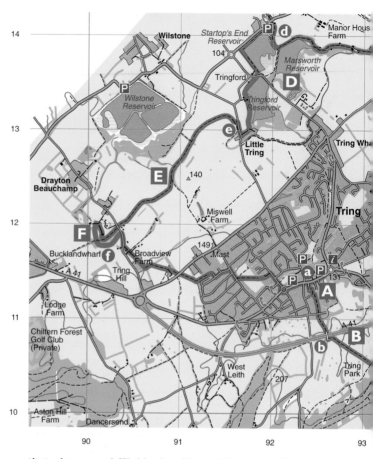

that also owned Waddesdon Manor, Mentmore Towers and other estates in Buckinghamshire. Rothschild transformed the house into a French Second Empire chateau, but most of the landscape park through which this route passes was laid out in the 18th Century, much by the great Charles Bridgeman in the 1720s when James Gibbs' obelisk and temple in the woods were also erected. In 1836 the great lime avenue, now so rudely interrupted by the A41 Tring by-pass, was planted.

b The bridge gives good views of Tring Park, framed by the 1836 lime avenue. Over the bridge, bear left to walk past the Woodland Trust information board through a fine 18th-Century landscaped park, in summer its pasture rich in wild flowers such as ladies bedstraw, nipplewort, vetch and hawkbit. Reaching the woods through a gate climb left towards Gibbs' stone obelisk in a beech hangar with yews.

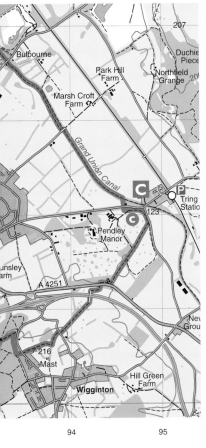

94   95

Beyond at the end of a vista between limes, yews and beeches is the pedimented and columned Ionic temple: both it and the obelisk have recently been well restored. Continue on the broad track to the temple, then follow the track round a sharp right bend to a gate. Turn left to another gate and join the Ridgeway Path. Follow it past Wigginton, and across the A41 on a high bridge. Beyond, the Path briefly follows the old Akeman Street line before turning left just past Beechtrees Cattery, the late 19th-Century south lodge to Pendley Manor, the path cutting through the estate with horse paddocks on the right, a dense belt of beech and sycamore on the left and a view of the Bridgwater Monument column above Aldbury ahead (Walk 29).

The earlier 18th century temple in Tring Park

Pendley Manor, now a country house hotel and conference centre, is a Victorian rebuild on the site of a village destroyed in 1440 by Sir Robert Wittingham to make a deer park. Emerging onto the road, follow it left to the junction with the Tring-Aldbury road and turn left to leave the Ridgeway Path. There is a glimpse of the canal to the right, then just before Ivy Cottage which has blue painted windows turn right at the footpath sign.

C The Grand Union Canal here is in a 30ft deep cutting as it passes through the highest part of its route through the Chilterns. Authorised by Act of Parliament in 1793 and originally built as the Grand Junction Canal, it reached and passed Tring in 1799 and opened fully in 1805.

c Pass to the right of Ivy Cottage garage and through a

Lock gates on the Grand Union Canal

copse into meadow. The canal in its deep cutting is invisible behind the thick hedge and scrub on the right of hawthorn, blackthorn and ash draped in clematis, black bryony and with blackberries ripening in the late summer months. To the left are superb meadows where a wealth of wild flowers might be seen including black medick, trefoils, marjoram, vetch, wild basil and scabious, while butterflies included peacocks, meadow browns, gatekeepers, marbled whites and whites. At a road a path ahead descends to the canal towpath, the canal still in a deep cutting. Alongside the canal there is herb robert, lesser burdock, bittersweet and great willowherb, while in the canal moorhens live.

Under Bridge 133 you pass the Bulbourne Works, the old canal company's major repair workshops and depot, now a British Waterways Depot. Mostly of about 1848, the architectural highlight is the ornate and weather-vaned late 19th-Century water tower. To the left of the canal is the Grand Junction Arms pub. From this point the canal begins its descent into the Vale of Aylesbury, the Marsworth Flight of seven locks which take the canal down 42ft (12.8m) in total. The locks have various dates on their abutments, mostly in the 1850s and 1860s, although the gates have been renewed many times since. The towpath passes the edge of the Marsworth Reservoir, its surface ruffled by the wind and with gulls and terns wheeling above it and its reeded margins. At Startop End, the last lock in the flight, there is a choice of refreshment: the Bluebells Tearoom with a rather good modern extension or White Lion pub.

D   The walk skirts three of the four reservoirs, dug by the Grand Junction Canal Company in the 1830s. They were used to supplement the water pumped from the leaky Wendover Arm to top up the main canal, which was depleted by the use of the Marsworth flight of locks.

d   Enter the Tring Reservoirs car park and climb the Startop's End reservoir's north embankment running parallel to the road. Walking west and south, cross the road at Tringford. Travel along the banks of Tringford Reservoir, a less exposed lake, the path winding through scrub willow, blackthorn, elm, hawthorn, sycamore and elder with a few horse chestnut trees while in the lake great crested grebe might be seen. Emerging from the wood veer slightly left over a stile to a road with Tringford Pumping Station ahead. This has dates on the buildings of '1803' and '1927' and had a steam powered beam engine in use until 1927 pumping water until replaced by a diesel engine. Continue down the lane, past barns converted to houses and past the Manor House, a good timber-framed building, to the road where you turn right and shortly turn left at a footpath sign onto a metalled track. Pass a gate and climb over a stile to join the towpath of the Wendover Arm branch of the Grand Junction Canal.

E   The Wendover Arm opened in 1797 and is just under seven miles long. Besides a barge trade it was intended as a feeder to the Tring summit, but it leaked from the start and on occasion even drew water away from the main canal. Consequently the four feeder reservoirs were dug and the exasperated canal authorities put in stop planks at Little Tring cutting it off from the main canal.

e   The footpath follows the old canal towpath for a mile and a half. The first half mile of the canal bed has been cleared in conjunction with works to extend the part of the canal holding water. However, the bed was drained in 1904 and much of it remains, sometimes full of poppies and rose bay willowherb, sometimes choked with thorn and blackthorn scrub and in other stretches a tangle of nettles and clematis. There are some good views from the canal, including to the north Mentmore Towers, another Rothschild mansion, and the canal company's fourth reservoir at Wilstone and now also a nature reserve. Passing beneath a cement rendered canal bridge, continue for a further 200 yards (183m) and turn right to scale the bank at a footpath sign to visit Drayton Beauchamp church.

Startop Farm from the canal reservoir embankment

F Drayton Beauchamp is a remarkably remote village that straggles away from the church. To the north of the church the trees straight ahead conceal a large moated site, now occupied by a modern house replacing the mansion pulled down in 1760. St Mary's has a chequered stone and flint nave and a banded ironstone and limestone chancel, all battlemented. Inside, the splendid Newhaven Monument of 1728 has his lordship reclining on a sarcophagus, her ladyship on a kind of shelf in front.

f Back at the canal, retraced your steps to the cement rendered bridge and ascend from the canal to follow the lane south and uphill, soon leaving it left onto the drive to Broadview Farm. Follow the footpath across horse paddocks before reaching the road past some chicken sheds. Across the road to the left of the lay-by climb a stile within the hedge. Diagonally left across the field, the path then passed to the right of a housing estate and to the left of a factory. This is Okeley Lane and the suburbs of Tring. Follow the estate road joined to its end at Miswell Lane, then left at a footpath sign through the recreation ground, skirting a school, Goldfield Infants School, to Christchurch Road where you turn right, then left at the crossroads back into the High Street.

A storm gathers over Wilstone Reservoir

ALDBURY

This route starts and finishes in the picturesque Hertfordshire village of Aldbury with its triangular green and pond, surrounded by good historic buildings. It also follows a stretch of the Grand Union Canal and climbs to the ridge behind Aldbury to the Bridgewater Monument, a column commemorating the 'Father of Inland Navigation', the pioneering canal building third Duke of Bridgewater.

A Aldbury is one of the most attractive villages in Hertfordshire, partly because of its setting with a tree-clad escarpment over 250ft (87m) high, hemming it in on the east side. The centre of the village is a triangular green with a pond and the village stocks. Around the green and along Stocks Road, which runs north from the green, there are many good houses, some timber-framed and jettied, such as Applegarth in Stocks Road and Manor Cottage behind the pond. There are also a number of good Georgian brick houses and Bridgewater estate cottages with the plaques with the letters 'LB' under a coronet. Near Manor Cottage a tall chimneyed building was erected as a communal bakehouse by the Bridgewater estate whose family seat was over the escarpment at Ashridge.

a From the car park in Stocks Road walk south to the village green and turn right to the church of St John the Baptist. To its right is the Victorian school with iron lattice casements and the LB monogram, as it was built by the Bridgewater estate. The church has a two-storey porch but has been refaced in Victorian restorations, but its chief glory lies within: in the south-east chapel is the Whittingham tomb of 1471 with effigies of Sir Robert in full armour and his wife. The chapel itself is enclosed by a 15th-Century stone screen still with its original tracery. In fact both screen and monument were brought from Ashridge in 1575.

Turn right out of the churchyard and just past it turn right through a kissing gate over a stile onto the Hertfordshire Way path, signed 'Pitstone Hill 1½ miles'. Beyond the paddock the path passes yellow brick 19th-Century farmbuildings to a kissing gate. Continue over one stile and through a metal kissing gate to cross a track, pausing to look back at the church tower and the Bridgewater Monument to the left. The

MAP:
HARVEY Route Map Ridgeway; OS Landranger Sheet 165, OS Explorer No 181 Chiltern Hills North

START/FINISH:
Car Park on Stocks Road, Aldbury SP965127. The 327 bus between Hemel Hempstead and Dunstable stops in Aldbury and Tring railway station is only a mile away, in fact nearer to Aldbury than it is to Tring

DISTANCE:
6 miles (9.5km)

APPROXIMATE TIME:
3 hours

HIGHEST POINT:
725ft (221m) at the Bridgewater Monument SP969131

REFRESHMENTS:
Aldbury has a range of facilities including the Greyhound Inn, the Town Farm Tea Rooms which also do lunches, and the Aldbury Village Store. At Cow Roast, near the Grand Union Canal lock, is the Cow Roast Inn

ADVICE:
The only route finding difficulty is after the Bridgewater Monument, and care is needed descending towards Aldbury, especially in wet conditions. As compensation there is a mile and a half of level canal walking

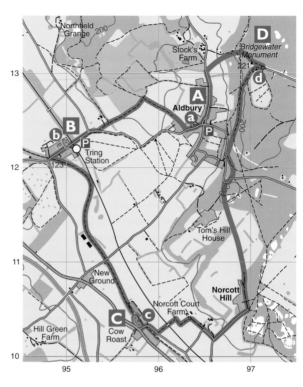

Jettied timber-framed cottages in Stocks Road, Aldbury

path ascends with a horse net and rail fence on the left and a thorn and blackthorn hedge on the right with lots of bindweed in flower. At a kissing gate and a footpath crossroads with a golf course beyond, turn left onto a path between hedges with splashes of colour provided by mallow, thistle and bramble flowers. Wild hops were everywhere and there was much knapweed, fumitory, lesser burdock, St John's wort and sorrel. The path is very nettly but this was compensated by a couple of wayfaring trees in full berry.

At a path junction join the Ridgeway Path and carry straight on to the road where you turn right to follow it past Tring Station.

B Tring Station is on the Euston line, built by the London to Birmingham Railway, reaching Tring in 1837 from London, and Birmingham in 1838, in the teeth of opposition from the local turnpike trusts and the Grand Junction Canal Company. The station itself has been rebuilt in modern style but the hotel built and opened in 1838 survives, as do a terrace of eleven railway workers' cottages beside it. The Royal Hotel, a hotel and posting house (for mail coach horses) is a large stucco building with a hipped slate roof, margined sashes and a Doric porch, now converted into houses and apartments.

b Walk past the old Royal Hotel and the terrace cottages towards the canal bridge, and leaving the Ridgeway Path cross the road onto the opposite side to descend to the canal towpath via steps. At the bottom of the steps turn sharp left to walk under the road bridge and along the Grand Union Canal towpath, the canal in its tree-lined cutting. Grey alder trees tower over the sycamores and ashes and in the verge are herb robert and bindweed. Follow the canal southwards and under Bridge 136. Ahead there were a lot of moored long boats as you approach Cow Roast Lock. A footbridge takes you over the access into Cow Roast Marina where numerous long boats are berthed and then reaching the lock and Bridge 137 which was rebuilt in 1914.

C Cow Roast is a curious name and refers to the golden days when there were acres of cattle pens used by cattle drovers from the Midlands en route to Smithfield and other London cattle markets. They put up in the Cow Roast Inn, the drovers that is, and today the pub is very popular and offers a chance for those following this route to pause for refreshment.

The Whittingham effigies seen through the stone screen, St John's Church, Aldbury

c You might want to watch long boats go through Cow Roast Lock. Leave the canal past the 1946 pump house to turn left on the lane and walk past the vehicle entrance to the Cow Roast Marina, then between thorn and elm hedges, possibly accompanied by comma, speckled wood and ringlet butterflies. Shortly, turn left at a footpath sign, the Chiltern Way, and over a stile in the hedge to cross a field to the footbridge over the railway and across another field. Through a hedge turn right, still on the Chiltern Way, and at the end turn right down the bridleway to the railway, turning left alongside it. At the bridle gate turn left out to the road and continue up the road to a T-junction and turn right. A sika deer and its two fawns watched me warily from the field as I passed, before springing into the trees.

At a second T-junction turn left onto the Icknield Way bridleway by the gates to Norcott Court, with the name on a slice of elm picked out in mosaic. The lane goes uphill with tall trees overhanging the road, including a cedar, pines, firs, oaks and beeches. The hedges are hazel, holly and hawthorn. At the top continue on the lane which turns left with beech woods on the right, part of the National Trust Ashridge estate.

On the Grand Union Canal

On the left are the plum brick walls to Norcott Hall, a neo-Georgian house. Further on are a 19th-Century barnyard, then a pair of estate cottages with steep pitched tiled roofs, all now converted to expensive residences.

Beyond, head for a pair of white painted gates. Cross a stile to the left of the two gates to walk along the left-hand side of a hedge through horse paddocks. The hedge is mostly blackthorn with a few oak standards and young sycamore and ash. Beyond the next field you pass the corner of Scrubs Wood which has oak, ash, cherry and black poplar trees. Through another field, this time along the right-hand side of the hedge, to a high galvanised kissing gate go almost straight on, on a clear path into a wood, which appears more heath than wood with bracken, oak, thorn, ash and silver birch. For the second time I stood eyeball to eyeball with a dark brown, almost black-coated sika deer. Before I could get my camera out she loped off through the scrub.

At the road turn right and walk along the bank above Grym's Dell. On reaching a road junction turn right and then left across the road to a track with a notice 'Restricted Access: Old Copse Lodge Only'. Walk along the track in mainly oak wood. At a bridleway sign turn left, shortly crossing another bridleway, the wood changing to beech on the slopes. Continue straight on across this bridleway down a track ahead with a 'No horses' sign. Follow this path downhill alongside a bridleway. The path soon follows the bank above a sunken way to the right with wire mesh fencing on the left and yews on both sides of the path. At a junction turn right to climb steeply uphill through a beech hanger on a chalky path with occasional steps. A path merges from the right; continue straight on, now on a hardened track, to the Bridgewater Monument, bending right in front of the Ashridge visitor centre to the end of the access road.

Cow Roast Lock

D The Bridgewater Monument was erected in 1832 to commemorate Francis, the third Duke of Bridgewater, the great canal pioneer or, as the inscription puts it 'The Father of Inland Navigation'. It is a tall fluted Doric column with a viewing platform and a copper urn. The base has a monumentality and sculptural quality worthy of Sir John Soane and the composition is superb. The viewing platform at the top is open from April to October in the afternoon, except Fridays, and is well worth the climb up the spiral staircase for the view.

The Bridgewater Monument

d Sometimes an ice cream van is at the top of the access road – or the nearby National Trust Visitor centre café is open afternoons except Fridays in the summer. It also has public toilets. From the access road, take the track to the right, where the track bends to the right of the Monument. Keep straight on ignoring a track to the right. Just before a cottage, turn half left onto a path past the right side of a large beech tree, shortly crossing a bridleway. Continue downhill on the path beyond the bridleway, accompanied by marbled white and peacock butterflies. The path joins a path from the left, turn right onto this and shortly turn left onto a steep path downhill by a notice 'Footpath to Aldbury'. Follow this waymarked path to a stile at the edge of the wood. Be very careful whilst descending this very steep path, it can be slippery in wet weather. Over the stile go diagonally left across the field to a second stile 100 yards (91.4m) to the left of the corner of the field. Turn right to a third stile out to the lane and turn left along the lane. You will shortly see a track on the right, turn right along the track and then almost immediately left onto a footpath through the hedge into the recreation ground and back to the car park.

IVINGHOE AND PITSTONE HILL

MAP:
HARVEY Route Map
Ridgeway; OS Landranger
Sheet 165, OS Explorer No
181 Chiltern Hills North

START/FINISH:
Car Park on Ridgeway Path
SP955149. There is no public
transport access to this car
park, although the Aylesbury
Luton service, No 61, stops
in Ivinghoe and there are
other routes including the
327 and 64 which go
through Ivinghoe

DISTANCE:
5½ miles (8.9 km)

APPROXIMATE TIME:
2½ hours

HIGHEST POINT:
702ft (214m) on Pitstone Hill
SP949142

REFRESHMENTS:
There are two pubs in
Ivinghoe, the King's Head
restaurant (which is rather
pricey) opposite the church
and the Rose and Crown in
Vicarage Lane which would
be my preference

ADVICE:
This walk is pretty
straightforward for route
finding and the climbs are
gradual. The car park can be
prone to car break-ins, as are
most along the Ridgeway
route and you may prefer to
rejig the walk to start in
Ivinghoe

This shortish walk follows one of the more open downland stretches of the Buckinghamshire section of the Ridgeway Path along Pitstone Hill which gives good views across the vale. It also includes a good stretch of Grim's Dyke, views of a 17th-Century post mill and the attractive village of Ivinghoe with its large 13th-Century church, as befits a former market town.

A The walk starts by climbing onto the ridge of Pitstone Hill, where recent scrub clearance has opened up the hillside. It is a reminder of the countryside around Grim's Ditch when the ditch was first dug and its embankment formed for this Iron Age linear earthwork. Recent excavations have shown that the Ditch was first dug in open arable country, which was then converted to grassland for hill pasture for Iron Age flocks. Presumably Grim's Ditch served to demarcate these pastures, heaths and commons from the arable below the scarp. It may even be that the area on the hills was used for communal pasture by the various estates and villages: a lot of work is still needed to put flesh on the bones of these mysterious linear earthworks. Most of Grim's Ditch that we have followed or crossed in the routes in this book have been in woodland which is not surprising as this conserves better than ploughing, but the stretch along the contours of Pitstone Hill give more of an idea of how the Ditch appeared to contemporaries, albeit with the bank then higher and the ditch deeper.

Grim's Ditch on Pitstone Hill

a   From the car park follow the Ridgeway Path south-west, that is on the car park side of the road. This is downland chalk pasture with a wide variety of wild flowers in the summer, including ladies bedstraw, trefoils, small and field scabious, agrimony, harebells, rest harrow, nippleworts, mouse-eared and other hawkweeds, clustered bellflowers, wild thyme, wild basil and self-heal. Butterflies include gatekeepers, meadow browns, ringlets, small heaths and whites. From Pitstone Hill look down over the site of the former Pitstone Cement Works, now closed and its buildings demolished, but a large lake or flooded pit remains. Where the scarp turns south Grim's Ditch appears and the Path follows the outer bank with the ditch on the left. The Path plunges into woodland beside a vast spreading beech tree via a kissing gate. Go through this gate and follow the Ridgeway sign into the wood. Much of the wood is open scrub with rose bay willowherb, wild hops and brambles. There is coppiced hazel and the woods are basically beech woods. Lesser burdock appears and bittersweet drapes the brambles. After a while, the path bears left past a Hertfordshire and Middlesex Wildlife Trust chalk downland restoration project and there is a further good stretch of Grim's Dyke. At the bottom of steps, turn sharp right to leave the Ridgeway Path at a footpath sign. Descend to a stile down a holloway with a footpath merging from the left. Follow the path that goes just inside the edge of the wood.

Pitstone Hill from the edge of Aldbury Nowers woods

The path crosses a track, then goes between hedges and fences to reach the road. At the road turn right to walk along the right hand verge with bindweed, vetch, knapweed, trefoil and rose bay willowherb growing in summer, the hedge draped in wild hop in yellowish flower. Ignore a footpath to the left and carry on until just past the gateway to Northfield Studios. On the right there is a footpath sign, which is easily missed, and go through a kissing gate. Turning left you are in a woodland strip parallel to the road and the path keeps within this belt of young sycamores and beeches behind the roadside hazel and thorn hedge. Many of the young trees have been 'barked' by deer.

Out of the wood over a stile, Folly Farm's barns have been converted to houses. Walk to the road junction bearing left and go straight over to a stile. Beyond this the path descends and

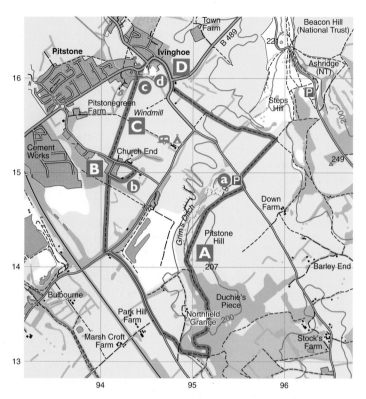

follows the left-hand side of a hedge, the field on the left being a former castle cement works chalk pit restored to level grassland. The pit on the right has also been restored. The path goes to the right of the hedge, with yellow-wort underfoot, then crosses the course of a dismantled quarry railway onto a path between chain link fences. At the time of writng there is a planning application for a factory access road to cross the path

Chalkstone 13th-Century stiff-leaf capitals in St Mary's Church, Ivinghoe

at GR941146. If successful, the footpath might change or cease to exist. At a lane turn right to the now- redundant St Mary's Church, Pitstone.

B Pitstone's medieval church with its battlemented tower and chancel, stands in splendid isolation, its churchyard amid arable fields and pastures. To the north across the lane is a large moated site which is probably the site of Pitstone place, a Jacobean mansion demolished in Victorian times. The village is a shrunken one, its centre of gravity having shifted to Pitstone Green further north-west, although Church Road was laid out by the Bridgewater estate in the mid 19th Century with cottages and a school that is now a house.

Pitstone Windmill

b Behind the church and in the left-hand wall of the churchyard, there is a wicket gate (hidden from view by a tall gravestone). Go through this gate, turn right and walk along the edge of an arable field. Climb a stile into the lane and turn left to walk past the entrance to Moat Farm on the right and past the end of Church Road on the left. Turn right through a kissing gate at a footpath sign for Ivinghoe, the path passing between arable fields with Ivinghoe church spire ahead. Crossing a track look right towards the isolated Pitstone Mill.

C Pitstone Windmill, now owned by the National Trust, is a post mill with some timbers dated 1627 and 1749. It has a weatherboarded upperwork on a 19th-Century brick ground storey. It looks remarkably archaic and is very similar to that at Brill, also in Buckinghamshire, of the 1680s. It was badly damaged in 1902 and was fully restored in the 1960s. It can be visited on Summer Sundays, accessed from south of Ivinghoe on the B488.

c Continue across the fields to a kissing gate, then go between gardens to emerge at the road by Green Lane House, a yellow brick house with Norfolk sashes, that is windows that slide sideways. Turning right walk uphill to the centre of Ivinghoe.

D Ivinghoe is a former market town: it received its royal charter in 1318 when the manor was held by the Bishop of Winchester. It certainly does not give the impression of being a town now, more a village, despite the grandeur of its church and the presence of a town hall. The latter appears as a timber-framed and jettied house with dormers, all of 1840s character. The best house in the centre is the Old Brewery House, now a Youth Hostel, of about 1800 with three storeys of sash

Steps Hill, Ivinghoe, seen across Incombe Hole

windows, those to the centre bay arched with a Doric doorcase. The King's Head opposite the church has cruck trusses in its carriageway fronting Station Road, while attached to the churchyard wall are a thatch hook and, rather gruesomely, a man trap. The hook is a long pole with a hook used for pulling burning thatch off a building: a rare survival. The church of St Mary is a large and most interesting one with 13th-Century transepts and a crossing tower crowned by a leaded spire, rather of the Hertfordshire spike style. Inside the nave arcade capitals are flowing 'stiffleaf' foliage carved in local chalk.

d   From the churchyard walk south down Church Road on a pavement to the B489 turning to Dunstable. Carry straight on along the B488, signposted to Tring with good views of Pitstone Mill to the right. After 50 yards (45.7m) or so leave the road over a stile onto a rather nettley footpath with good views to the left towards the bare downs of Ivinghoe Beacon.

The path begins a gradual climb towards the Chiltern escarpment, initially alongside crops with a hedge on the left, then through pasture, part of it a chalk grassland restoration project by MAFF. Go diagonally across a narrow meadow, through a hedge and over a stile and then through crops with field forget-me-nots, poppies and knotgrass and common fumitory on the path in summer. The path skirts Incombe Hole, a deep curving combe to the left cut into the escarpment. Over a stile and into pasture, turn right and walk alongside a fence to the Ridgeway Path where you turn right through a kissing gate to follow it along the ridge to the road and the car park. It was here that I disturbed a yellowhammer drinking from a puddle.